Sixties American Cars

Dan Lyons

Motorbooks International
Publishers & Wholesalers

To Catherine, James, and Joyce Robin,
with love

First published in 1998 by Motorbooks International
Publishers & Wholesalers, 729 Prospect Avenue,
PO Box 1, Osceola, WI 54020-0001 USA

Motorbooks International books are also available at
discounts in bulk quantity for industrial or sales-
promotional use. For details write to Special Sales
Manager at the Publisher's address

Printed in Hong Kong through World Print, Ltd.

Library of Congress Cataloging-in-Publication Data
    Lyons, Dan.
    Sixties American cars/Dan Lyons.
        p. cm.—(Enthusiast color series)
    Includes index.
    ISBN 0-7603-0327-4 (paperback: alk. paper)
    1. Automobiles—United States—History. 2. Automobiles
    —United States—Pictorial works. I. Title. II. Series.
    TL23.L96   1998
    629.222'0973'09046—dc21   97-43431

On the front cover: Chevrolet's Impala first
appeared in 1958 and instantly became a modern-day
classic. This 1962 Impala convertible, owned by
International Motorcars of Distinction, is powered by
Chevy's legendary 409 V-8 engine.

On the frontispiece: The front fenders on Glenn
Hutchinson's 1969 Corvette feature fender slots
dressed with optional trim liners. The Stingray
nameplates, which weren't on the 1968 models,
returned in 1969.

On the title page: Beyond the venomous Cobra,
Carroll Shelby lent his considerable expertise and well-
known name to another Ford venture in the 1960s.
Between 1965 and 1970, a high-performance variant
of Ford's fledgling pony star appeared, bearing the
name of this American racing legend—the Shelby
Mustang. This 1969 Shelby is owned by Hank
D'Amico.

On the back cover: The 1969 Dodge Charger R/T
retained the clean, classic body lines of the totally
restyled 1968 Charger. Subtle exterior changes for
1969 included a split grille and redesigned taillights.
This red-hot Charger R/T belongs to Tom Pellegrino.

Contents

Acknowledgments

My thanks to all of the car owners whose vehicles appear in this book for their courtesy and cooperation in allowing me to photograph them. The cars and their owners are listed below, not necessarily in the order of their appearance.

1967 Mercury Cougar Dan Gurney Edition, Fred Scheer

1964 Mercury Comet Cyclone, David Duffee

1963 Ford Falcon convertible, Ralph Tomlin

1963 Pontiac Grand Prix, George Munsterman

1965 Olds 88 convertible, Joe Bawduniak

1964 Cadillac Eldorado convertible, John Kepich

1967 Pontiac Firebird convertible, Lindsay Carte

1968 Chevy Yenko Camaro, Golden Classics

1969 Chevy Impala Custom Sport Coupe, Jim and Stan Biernacki

1960 Cadillac Eldorado convertible, Jerry Lambert

1966 Olds 4-4-2, Bud Congrove

1969 Chevy Corvette, Glenn Hutchinson

1960 Studebaker Champ, Ken Anderson

1964 Chevy Corvair convertible, Wilbur Groesbeck

1966 Chevy El Camino, Ron Moore

1957 DeSoto Fireflite, Glenn and Barbara Patch

1979 Dodge Li'l Red Express Truck, Harry Magnuson

1968 Ford Ranchero, Karl Yager

1967 Ford Fairlane and 1964 Ford Galaxie 500, Larry Axley

1966 Ford Mustang convertible, Jim Boniello

1964 1/2 Ford Mustang convertible, Tara McCoy

1966 Ford Mustang Fastback, Andrew Esposito

1969 Shelby GT350 convertible, Hank D'Amico

1963 Ford Thunderbird, Chuck Ziska

1969 Plymouth Barracuda convertible, Joe and Ann Sala

1960 Chrysler 300F convertible, Jarvis Barton

1965 Buick Skylark Gran Sport, Ron Berry

1963 Pontiac Bonneville convertible, Dave and Cindy Keetch

1969 Pontiac Grand Prix SJ, Russ Catalano

1962 Chevy Impala SS convertible, International Motorcars of Distinction

1969 Dodge Charger 500, Mike Russo

1968 Chrysler Imperial Crown convertible, John Kepich

1965 Chrysler 300L convertible, T.J. Manganello

1966 Plymouth Satellite convertible and 1963 Plymouth Savoy, Chuck Bubie

1968 Dodge Charger R/T, Angela DePasquale

1969 Dodge Charger R/T, Tom Pellegrino

1964 Plymouth Sport Fury, Ray Elias

1963 Studebaker Avanti, Lloyd Watts

1961 Studebaker Lark convertible, Sam Cannato

1962 Studebaker Hawk GT, John Reichard

1969 AMC Hurst Scrambler, Adrian Brooks

1969 AMC AMX California Special, Victor and Barbara Nave

1965 Pontiac GTO, Lindsay Carte

1967 Lincoln Continental convertible, Rich Battistoni

1969 Ford Torino Talladega and 1963 Ford Galaxie Lightweight, Dick Kainer

—Dan Lyons

1

Farewell to the 1950s

Like a class of wild high school seniors, 1950s cars had some notable characters. If there had been a yearbook for the decade, the 1957 Chrysler 300 might have been voted "most likely to exceed (the speed limit)," and Ford's innovative but erratic retractable hardtops of 1957 to 1959 would have been the easy choice for "least likely to recede." The 1957 Ford Thunderbird was the prom queen, while the 1955 Chevy Bel Air convertible would have undoubtedly held the "most-likely-to-have-someone-say-they-had-one-just-like-it-but-it-was-a-four-door-and-it-wasn't-a-convertible-and-I-think-it-was-a-Plymouth" award.

The early 1950s spawned both styling trends (pillarless hardtop construction, for example) and mechanical developments (such as the high-compression, overhead-valve V-8) that would become integral parts of the American automotive scene for years to come. The mid-1950s brought more innovation (e.g., Chevy's legendary small-block V-8), sweet two-seaters (such as the Corvette and T-Bird), and an explosion of two- and three-tone color schemes. And as the decade began to wind down, ever-larger tail fins sprouted throughout the industry and shot out in all directions.

The year 1957 just might have been the peak of 1950s styling and performance. A bumper crop of cars destined to become classics were produced that year: Chevy's Bel Air and fuel-injected Corvette, Ford's last little Thunderbird, Studebaker's supercharged Golden Hawk, and Chrysler's elegant brute, the 300-C, to name but a few.

A deep recession ravaged the U.S. economy in 1958, and red ink ran over the balance sheets of virtually all auto makers (save the compact car specialists at Rambler). On the heels of the recession, car makers seemed unsure of themselves; styling went from wild to outright bizarre, with tail fins reaching new heights (or depths) and chrome trim festooned almost everywhere.

Then the final bell for the decade rang and the class of the 1950s burst out the doors into the future. As if in response to the wildness of their recent past, early 1960s cars grew more conservative, more

Farewell to fins. The most famous 1950s styling icon was the tail fin, here exemplified by the 1957 DeSoto Fireflite. Born late in the 1940s, tail fins peaked (so to speak) in the late 1950s only to become quickly passé as the next decade arrived. Cadillac, which had started it all back in 1948, was among the last to give them up. By the mid-1960s, they had sunk back into the fenders from whence they'd sprung.

practical. Car building is nothing if not cyclical, though, and within a few years the sensible economy cars were joined by thoroughly impractical (and *fun, fun, fun*) intermediate-sized cars packed full of engine. The more aggressive they were the better they sold, and Detroit soon learned the lesson. By the end of the decade some of the neon colors and in-your-face graphics being offered could make anything from the 1950s seem almost understated.

The 1950s gave us styling successes and excesses, technological innovation, and incredi-

bly uneven build quality—the latter a fact that's often forgotten through the haze of memory and the skills of modern-day restorers. But because this period also spanned the childhood of so many baby boomers, we've wrapped it in a protective cloth of nostalgia. Look a little harder, and you can see the 1950s as an automotive age that was both amazing and awful. Early conservatism gave way to growing liberalism and a decade-ending crescendo, a pattern the 1960s would prove to repeat.

2

Ford Motor Company

The 1950s had been a memorable decade for Ford Motor Company. In that ten-year span, the company bested arch-rival Chevy twice in model year sales (1954 and 1957), celebrated its fiftieth anniversary (in 1953), and bid farewell to the fabled flathead V-8 (replaced by the Y-block eight in '54). The sporty, new Thunderbird appeared in 1955 and promptly showed its tail feathers to Chevy's Corvette for each of the three years that the two-seaters competed directly in the marketplace. T-Bird got bigger in 1958 and so did its sales, and the personal luxury cars went on to be a mainstay in the lineup. Not so Edsel. The cars with the horse collar grille made their debut in the midst of 1958's bone-shaking recession.

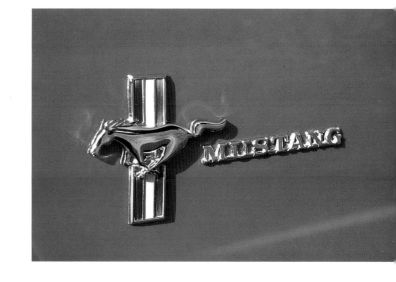

If ever there was a case for not fixing something that wasn't broken, the 1966 Mustang was it—in just its second year of production, the Mustang had already sold its one-millionth car. Ford had the sense to leave well enough alone, limiting the changes for 1966 to things like new rocker-panel moldings, standard back-up lights, and slightly reworked grille and gas-cap designs. Inside, all 1966s got the circular five-dial instrument panel formerly reserved for the costlier GT.

The mid-priced Edsel was unconventional and upscale—a combination that did not sit well with the few recession-rattled car buyers who were actually shopping in '58. The economy recovered but Edsel never did, disappearing quietly in 1960.

Early in the 1950s, Lincoln made an unlikely name for itself in auto racing. Specially prepared

An astounding 680,989 Mustangs were built in its extended first year, 1965. Aside from the genius of driving a sporty little tap into a monstrous keg of buyers, another key to the Mustang's success was its flexibility. Thanks to an arm's-length option list, buyers could spec the cars out from mild to wild.

Lincolns dominated their class in the grueling Mexican Road Races, notching at least first and second every year from 1952 to 1954. Late in the decade, America's growing interest in smaller automobiles made for painful times for luxury marques like Lincoln. Sandwiched in the middle, Continental officially parted from parent Lincoln as a separate make, most notable for producing the Mark II—a beautiful, impeccably built luxury coupe with a mind-blowing price tag of 10,000 1956 dollar bills. Though Lincoln reportedly lost about $1,000 on every car, it might have been worth it for the luster that the Mark brought upon the company.

Meanwhile, Mercury cruised through the early 1950s, building up to a smashing sales year peak in 1955–56 before sliding downward as the decade drew to a close. Following on the (winged) heels of its mid-1950s success, Mercury celebrated in '57 with its first ever unique body shells and chassis. Unfortunately, buyers greeted them with only tepid applause. Not surprisingly, the exodus of buyers from the mid-size field in the wake of 1958's recession did little good for a company who specialized in mid-sized cars—like Mercury. Sales would not rebound until Mercury followed the industry lead and down-sized their products in the early 1960s.

The 1960s brought plenty of interesting products out of Dearborn. Lincoln's Continental merged elegant styling and unparalleled build quality. Small, sporty, and easy to personalize, the Ford Mustang scratched an itch that most car buy-

13

ers didn't even know they had before it arrived in 1964. Ford's Thunderbird continued to fly upscale from its early sporting roots, uncovering some personal luxury milestones and later in the decade, losing its way. The Mercury Cougar was based on the wildly successful Mustang and offered a stylish counterpoint to the first pony car. The Ford Falcon appeared in 1960 and became the first compact car by the Big Three to enjoy wide-scale success in the 1960s. And finally, Ford and Mercury contributed their share to the industry's decade-long horsepower race.

Ford Mustang
Horses for Courses

The Mustang was a marketing masterpiece. Small, sporty cars were already selling well by the early 1960s, but when the stylish 2+2 appeared in the spring of 1964, well, this was something else entirely. Hundreds of thousands of buyers fell in love with it overnight. The Mustang had the right price, right performance, right styling, and it made the right statement.

If one car is synonymous with the 1960s, it's the Mustang. Formally introduced on April 17, 1964, at the New York World's Fair, the pioneering pony car came thundering out of the paddock to trample Ford's prerelease first-year sales estimate of 100,000. By the time the corral gate was hitched at the end of an extended 1965 model year, a record-setting 680,989 had been saddled up and sold.

Credit for conjuring up the Mustang generally goes to Lido "Lee" Iacocca, then the head of Ford Division and later the high-profile savior of Chrysler Corporation. In truth, the car was created by a host of Ford stylists, planners, and marketers, but Iacocca was the vocal front-man and champion of this right

product for the right market at the right time. The Mustang filled a need that its buyers didn't even know they had yet.

First and foremost, the car was about *style*. Its long-hood/short-deck raciness and 2+2 seating soon became the core components of the "pony car" look, and variations on this theme would grace the most collectible cars of the 1960s. Another key to its popularity was the length of its option list— Mustangs could be optioned from mild to wild, depending on the buyer's tastes and pocketbook— and everyone from drag racers to little old ladies found one to their liking.

A third factor in the Mustang's favor, especially early on, was its lack of competition. GM, Chrysler, and AMC were caught with their corporate pants down and it took them a few years to catch up—of course, some interesting products were pressed into service as makeshift Mustang fighters until the genuine articles could be finished. In March 1966, less than two years after the car's official debut, the one-millionth Mustang rolled off the assembly line.

Post-1967, Mustang sales started to dip. Though more than 474,000 were built that year, the total represented a slide of almost 25 percent from previous levels. The falloff had a simple cause: The Mustang wasn't the only game in town anymore, as newcomers such as the Camaro and Firebird joined with newly competitive veterans like the Barracuda.

Another factor in the Mustang's inexorable slide from the top was the rapid rise of the musclecar class. By the mid-1960s, the practice of putting a high-performance V-8 into an intermediate (or smaller) class car was widespread. Every manufacturer was taking its fastest engine and its best shoehorn and creating new performance cars from the lightest model in its lineup capable of swallowing heavy V-8 iron. But while this trend added competitive models to the field, the Mustang was flexible enough to swallow

Built to plug the growing gap between the compact Falcon and full-sized Galaxie, Ford's Fairlane appeared in 1962 at the right place and right time. The intermediate's not-too-big/not-too small strategy racked up 297,000 first-year sales.

powerful engines of its own, giving it legitimate credibility in the muscle-car field as well.

The Mustang remains a survivor. Through the dark days of the early 1970s and into the early 1980s—when precious little of interest was manufactured by *anybody*—the Mustang hung on, spinning off endless variations on the pony car theme. Some, like the Pinto-based Mustang II, died the death they de-served; others, such as the well-balanced Mustang SVO, expired before their time. And some (the reborn 5.0 V-8s of the late 1980s/early 1990s) went on to define the rebirth of the muscle-car class. Like the Camaro and Firebird, the Mustang managed to adapt and survive without losing its essential mission: being fun to drive.

15

Lincoln Continental

Quality Was Job One

Popular then, popular now: Lincoln Continentals were good sellers in the 1960s (and the years since), and the convertibles in particular have become blue-chip collectibles. These luxurious open cars combine excellent quality, limited-production exclusivity, and the added flair of top-down motoring.

It was the finest Lincoln built in the 1960s. It was one of the best postwar designs to emerge from any auto maker. And it was almost a Thunderbird.

As the story goes, in 1958, Ford Division boss Robert S. McNamara saw a styling study under consideration for the third-generation 1961 Thunderbird. McNamara—who later became secretary of defense under President John F. Kennedy—thought the styling was too formal for the sporty T-Bird, but just the ticket for the new 1961 Lincolns. McNamara promptly asked his designers to do the improbable: transform the two-door Thunderbird mockup into a four-door Lincoln Continental—*in two weeks*.

The Continental convertible's elaborate top mechanism (this one's a 1967) was descended from that of the retractable-hardtop Ford of the late 1950s. A daunting mass of relays, motors, hydraulics, and pivot links, it continues to bemuse mechanics to this day. Before installation, each Continental's 430-inch V-8 would be run on the bench, torn down, inspected, and re-assembled.

Amazingly, they did it. In fact, when the new Lincoln appeared for 1961, it proved to be quite faithful to these earliest design studies. Credited to Elwood P. Engel's studio, the car's elegant, square-shouldered theme wore well for Lincoln throughout the decade and beyond.

After all the lumpy, disjointed exuberance of the 1958–1960 Lincolns, the 1961 "stiletto-look" Continentals were wonderfully simple. Slab-sided and symmetrical, their clean, uncomplicated details and daring suicide doors harked back to a purer era. The Continentals were beautiful, and beautifully built. In an era when American cars weren't known for careful assembly, Continentals were notable exceptions. Every engine was bench-tested for three hours at 3,500 rpm, followed by disassembly, inspection, and re-assembly.

Bodies were blasted with water, and dye was run through the oil to detect leaks. And if the cars passed muster, they were then given a 12-mile road test. Lincoln kept 16 full-time staff members busy evaluating cars before delivery, and their confidence was shown in their warranty: Lincoln backed the Continental with a then-unheard-of two-year/ 24,000-mile guarantee.

Even so, if these extraordinary measures had one purpose in mind—to knock Cadillac from the top of the luxury-car heap—they weren't enough. By the end of the 1960s, Lincoln's arch rival was still the market leader. But Lincoln had a decade of strong showings to be proud of, and the company earned its newfound status honorably: by building some of the highest-quality cars the country had ever seen.

When the Thunderbird left the two-seater ranks after 1957 it created a self-defined new category—the "personal luxury" class. Four-place Square Birds of 1958–1960 were followed up with the equally distinctive Bullet Bird style of 1961–1963. This 1963 hardtop coupe had a base sticker price of $ 4,445.

Ford Thunderbird
Flying First Class

The Thunderbird was the automotive Elvis. Bursting on the scene in the mid-1950s as a lean and racy thriller, it gradually got more mainstream and conservative as time went on. By the 1970s, this once-lithe performer was bloated, bulky, and had thoroughly lost its way. But unlike the King, the T-Bird would live to rise again. Recreating itself in the early 1980s as a sleek, aerodynamic 2+2, Ford's personal coupe eventually regained some of the strut of its good ol' days.

Few cars have undergone as much transformation as this one. Consider the first T-Birds: Hatched for a 1955 debut, these sporty two-seaters were an instant hit. The Thunderbird wildly outsold its

crosstown rival, the Corvette, for the three years in which they were direct competitors, 1955 to 1957. Timeless styling has made these small Birds a perennial 1950s icon and one of the decade's true blue-chip collectibles.

Yet even as these cars were winning style points and their market segment, Ford was planning to make the little Birds a little bigger. Dearborn knew that most buyers wanted four seats rather than two, so for 1958 the second-genera-

The Cougar was well received by the public and the press when it arrived in 1967. First-year sales reached 150,000, and *Motor Trend* named it the Car of the Year. To capitalize on its Trans-Am relationship with popular driver Dan Gurney, starting in 1967 Mercury offered a Cougar trim package called the Dan Gurney Special. Features included turbine wheel covers over F70 wide-oval whitewalls, a chromed engine dress-up kit, and decals of Dan's signature applied to the rear quarter windows.

tion T-Bird arrived with rear seats, a much larger platform, and radical new styling. These "Square Birds" marked not only the end of the elegant two-place T-Birds, they also created a whole new niche—the personal luxury class.

However much enthusiasts might have regretted it, Ford's hunch proved right on the money and Thunderbird profits soared. Sales of the second-generation (1958-1960) Thunderbirds dwarfed the three-year run of the two-seaters (198,192 versus 53,166). And when the third-generation Birds made their debut in 1961, it was clear that Ford had pulled off a rare automotive hat trick: three successive styling winners in a row. The 1961-1963 Thunderbird was still a big personal-luxury coupe, but smooth, torpedo-like lines replaced the angular jauntiness of the Square Birds. In a nod to Birds past, a two-seat variation even appeared in 1962: the Sport Roadster. This transformation was managed by means of a sleek fiberglass tonneau that started at the rear deck and swept up into the headrests of the front seats.

The fourth- and fifth-generation cars arrived in 1964 and 1967, respectively, and both mirrored the personal development of many potential buyers: They got heavier, softer, and more conservative. Ford figured that any buyers wanting smaller and sportier cars could be accommodated elsewhere in the lineup, so 1967 also marked the first year for a four-door variant and the first without a convertible. Through the late 1960s the T-Bird at least retained a certain dignity and style; soon thereafter, though, serious middle-age spread set in. For the Thunderbird, as for most American cars, the 1970s was a rather lost decade. Fortunately, redemption was at hand in 1983 with the introduction of a smaller, sportier Bird. As of this writing Ford is predicting the T-Bird's demise—stand-alone RWD platforms have become awfully costly these days. But even if the current Bird goes away, plans are afoot to reinvent it once more near the turn of the century—and this time, perhaps, as something closer to the original model's concept.

Mercury Cougar
Pony cars on the European Plan

Though the original Cougar was based on the Mustang platform, it would be a mistake to think of it as just a horse of a different color. By virtue of its deft design and execution, Mercury's sophisticated pony car became one of the most interesting cars of the 1960s.

Given the Mustang's wild success, it was natural that Ford Division would have to share the wealth. Right on cue, two-plus years after the Mustang's debut, Mercury unveiled its own pony car.

Given Mercury's place in the Ford/Lincoln/Mercury triumvirate, it was no surprise that the 1967 Cougar entered the fray slightly upscale from the Mustang. Elegant styling helped make that distinction clear. Mercury's big cat took the traditional long-hood/short-deck pony car stance and turned it into a remarkably graceful shape: long, low, and Euro-looking in its lack of excess trim. Crisp, contoured sides blended into a bold nose and tail, and the centered insignia up front split two clean sets of ribbed, hideaway headlights.

The Cougar was initially available in base and GT versions, with a dressier XR-7 package coming online midway through the first season. In the next few years, the menu became more varied—practically every performance engine in Ford's arsenal fit nicely in the engine bay, and most found their way onto the option sheet. A convertible joined the lineup in 1969 and stuck around until 1974.

Cougar made a nice splash when it arrived in 1967, racking up more than 150,000 units in its first year. Production tailed off after that, in no small measure due to the ever-increasing glut of pony and musclecar rivals. Unlike many of its contemporaries, the Cougar survived well into the 1990s. During this run, it clawed its way through the 1970s and re-emerged further upscale in 1983 as a more luxurious notchback version of the redesigned Thunderbird.

The Fairlane scooped the competition in popularizing the intermediate-sized car, but a couple of years later it was GM that discovered the niche's secret. Largely due to its desperate need for an image booster, for 1964 Pontiac stuffed a full-sized V-8 into the midsized Tempest Le Mans, called it a GTO, and created the 1960s musclecar. Ford couldn't fight back until the redesigned Fairlane arrived for 1966—the existing car's engine bay was too tight for a big-block. When the second-generation Fairlane arrived, it had room for any engine in Ford's arsenal. That and its cleaner, meaner looks convinced more than 317,000 buyers to park one in their driveway—a boost of 42 percent over 1965. This Springtime Yellow 1967 Fairlane 500 is one of precious few street models built with Ford's 427-inch, 425-brake horsepower R-code V-8.

Nineteen sixty-three was the first year for the open-air Falcon, which came in both standard and sporty Sprint versions. This 1963 was one of 31,192 standard convertibles built that year, which was also the last for the first-generation Falcon. The friendly, rounded form gave way in 1964 to a blander, squarer shape.

Ford Falcon
Simple Sells

For a brief time in the late 1950s, America's independents had the compact market all to themselves. That all changed at the end of the 1950s, when the Big Three launched small, entry-level platforms of their own. What the Valiant was to Chrysler and the Corvair was to Chevrolet, so the Falcon was to Ford.

Ford's entry into the fledgling compact market at the beginning of the 1960s was the Falcon. Unlike the Corvair, it was a straightforward little car with an unassuming design and a user-friendly mechanical layout. Despite—or more likely because of—this, the Falcon easily beat its Big Three competitors in sales, booking 435,676 units in its first model year.

The Falcon's early success came in equal parts from its basic good value and the market's general doubts about the other new compacts. The Corvair featured a radical air-cooled rear-engine layout while

23

Comet

America's newest compact car styled like a fine car— priced with or below other compacts

LOOKS LIKE A MILLION, RUNS ON PENNIES, TURNS ON A DIME

Styling with a fine-car flair. Comet brings a new, perfectly balanced design to the compact car field. There's a refreshing, jaunty look in every crisp line. **The low price is a wonderful surprise.** The Comet looks far more expensive than it is. Though it is obviously a superior value, Comet is priced with or below other compacts like Rambler, Corvair, Lark and Valiant. **Comet is thrifty with gas.** The new Thrift Power Six delivers up to 28 m.p.g. of regular gas. You'll save with every tankful. And Comet's longer wheelbase (114″ instead of the average 107″) gives you the smoothest ride in its field.

Comet is generous with extras. Dual headlights, front and rear arm rests, door-operated dome light, fine fabrics, handsome appointments and many more extras are yours at no extra charge in Comet. **Comet offers two wonderful wagons.** The full line includes a two- and a four-door station wagon. The cargo space is 76 cubic feet BIG and the rear window is retractable for better ventilation, easier loading. Choice of smart, decorator-planned interiors—stunning exteriors. Compare all the compact cars—and you'll come away with a Comet. **See Comet at your Mercury-Comet dealer's now.**

LINCOLN-MERCURY DIVISION *Ford Motor Company.* BUILDERS OF FINER CARS OF EVERY SIZE FOR EVERY PURPOSE

LINCOLN AND LINCOLN CONTINENTAL—THE ULTIMATE IN MOTOR CARS • MERCURY—THE *BETTER* LOW-PRICE CAR • COMET—FIRST OF THE COMPACT CARS WITH FINE-CAR STYLING

Ford and Mercury had the right product for the times in their Falcon and Comet. Introduced in mid-model year 1960, a basic Comet four-door stickered for $2,053 while the wagon weighed in at $2,365. The Comet joined its corporate Falcon cousin to do battle with Chevy's Corvair, Studebaker's Lark, Plymouth's Valiant, and Rambler's American in the fledgling compact class. Traditional design and engineering likely helped the Comet/Falcon take an easy sales win over the Corvair, which featured a seemingly radical air-cooled rear engine.

sales of the Corvair, Ford followed suit in 1961 with the racier Falcon Futura. A convertible was added in 1963, as well as the Falcon Sprint—a sporty, V-8-powered offshoot that could back up its bucket seats with honest performance. Ultimately, this market would be mined to perfection by the Mustang, which was based almost entirely on the existing Falcon floor pan.

The years 1964 and 1965 saw a second-generation Falcon with a new, more angular, and arguably less attractive body. The next (and final) generation moved up the size scale and was little more than a sawed-off version of Ford's intermediate-sized Fairlane. While the Falcon continued to serve well in this guise, its sales tailed off later in the decade. The Falcon's last year was 1970, after which the equally compact Maverick, which arrived the same year, took its role.

the conventionally built Valiant sported distinctly *unconventional* styling. Ford's entry was the most mainstream in both looks and engineering, and as such it appealed to the same conservative, frugal mindset that defined the compact buyer.

Offered initially as a two- or four-door sedan or station wagon, all models had a base 144-inch straight-six good for 90 horsepower. But when Chevy found that sporty-ish features did wonders for

Mercury's Comet and Ford's Falcon were friendly, straightforward, economical cars hatched with few performance aspirations. Sportier versions of both soon emerged in the form of the Falcon Sprint and Comet Cyclone. Powered by Ford's trusty 289 V-8, these models' growing reputation in rally racing gave owners something to brag about besides their mileage figures. This 1964 Comet Cyclone was first owned by a Long Beach woman who bought it on Valentine's Day 1964 and owned it for the next 17 years.

Ford Performance

*Fast Horses, Quick Cats, and other
Performance Notables*

Over the years, just about every automotive manufacturer has had an occasional flirtation with racing. In reality, the benefits to consumers have usually been little more than bragging rights—but when it comes to showroom sales, what a benefit that often proves! Ford has learned this lesson even better than most, and some of its most exciting products of the 1960s wore a proud costume from the racetrack.

Throughout the 1960s, Ford Motor Company was convinced that racing was good for business. Covertly at first and blatantly later on, Ford sponsorship and research led to major competition successes. Perhaps no other manufacturer has enjoyed the diversity of success that Ford reaped in this decade: Le Mans, NASCAR, Indy, drag strips, and more all saw victories for the blue oval.

You could argue that it all began in Mexico. For three straight years in the early 1950s, Lincoln won the American Stock class in the Carrera Panamericana—also called the Mexican Road Race. Lincoln faded from competition after that, but the taste of

To keep pace at the drag strip in 1963, Ford took a time-honored two-part approach: add muscle and lose weight. The brawn came from the all-new 427 big-block, the slim-down via a factory lightweight program. Select sheet metal was swapped for fiberglass or aluminum, and every nonessential part was scuttled. Veteran racer Dick Brannan campaigned two such Galaxies in 1963, including the one you see here. Along the way Brannan notched the NHRA Super Stock title. While the following generation of Galaxies would be slimmer and stronger, they were still no lightweights—which is why Ford dropped the 427 into the intermediate-sized Fairlane for its next drag strip brawler, the legendary Thunderbolt.

Slick-looking fastbacks like this 1966 were latecomers to the Mustang lineup. The notchback and convertible made their official debut in April 1964, but the 2+2 fast-back didn't join the lineup until the following fall.

success—and the all-important experience and personnel—lingered on for FoMoCo.

Mercury's Cougar had a moment in the sun as well, running credibly in the SCCA Trans-Am

Ford's entire line-up won Motor Trend's 1964 Car of the Year award. Though full-sized Galaxies like this 500XL hardtop were by then in the last year of their styling cycle, they still did well on the sales floor and the race track. In all, Ford picked up 30 wins in NASCAR and sold more than 593,000 Galaxie 500s.

series (with drivers such as Dan Gurney, Parnelli Jones, and Peter Revson) in 1967 and the NASCAR ovals in 1968, where Cougars bagged 10 out of 19 GT-class wins.

But of all the Dearborn contingent, Ford would naturally make the biggest splash in racing. When the V-8 Falcon Sprint appeared late in the 1963 model year, the car proved just fast and rugged enough to make an excellent rally racer. That year Falcons took first and third in class, second overall

The Torino Talladega was one of several 1960s performance cars that owed its existence entirely to racing. In order to qualify a new car for NASCAR's Grand National circuit, a manufacturer had to build 500 units for sale to the public. Ford beat that easily, producing some 754 Talladegas in all, including prototypes. A longer snout, flush-fitting grille, and sleeker fastback tail made the Talladegas a touch more aerodynamic than the standard Torinos, which translated into real benefits on NASCAR's high-speed ovals. Street versions like this Presidential Blue model used the 428 Cobra Jet, while racers first packed a 427 and later Ford's 429.

at the prestigious Rallye Monte Carlo—an astounding feat in that bastion of European GTs. Falcons continued flying high in the sport for years.

By this time, however, Ford was already maneuvering behind the scenes to become a racing powerhouse. The corporate prez, Henry Ford II, officially took the gloves off in 1962, declaring that the company would no longer abide by the so-called AMA Racing Ban of 1957, the Big Three's voluntary agreement to avoid factory-backed competition. Ford, Chrysler, and GM had all supported racing covertly anyway, but Dearborn was the first to take it aboveboard.

Ford's abortive effort to purchase Italian super-car builder Ferrari, which blew up in 1963, leaving tempers hot on both sides, left HFII determined to beat Enzo at his own game, specifically endurance racing. Ford turned instead to English carmaker Lola and acquired the rights to the revolutionary Lola GT, a midengined sports prototype carrying the new thin-wall Ford V-8. Lola's experience quickly led Ford into its own GT40, and though the costly program stumbled at first, it eventually led to a stunning four-year string of wins at Le Mans (1966 to 1969). Even after Ford's official withdrawal from endurance racing after 1967, the Ford-backed Cosworth V-8 kept the name in Europe's top echelon.

On the domestic front, huge kudos were earned at the Indy 500. After countless years as an also-ran, Ford finally broke through at the Brickyard in 1965, winning the top-four places. More wins came in 1966 and 1967. And of course the Mustang's track success seems almost predictable, given its sporting pretensions and made-for-modifying personality. The circuit where Mustangs really sparkled was the SCCA Trans-Am, where Dearborn clinched the manufacturer's title in 1966, 1967, and 1970. Mustangs also thundered their way to success in club racing, rallying, and drag racing.

Needless to say, any book covering Ford in the 1960s would be remiss if it didn't pay homage to the legendary Carroll Shelby. This talented Texan first gained fame in the 1950s as one of the country's best—and most watchable—sports-car drivers. Three national championships and an overall victory at Le Mans (for Aston-Martin in 1959) were just the highlights of a brilliant driving career.

Acute angina had forced Shelby into retirement by the early 1960s, so the slick-talking Texan set out for new challenges. He soon hit on a hybrid of Eng-land's AC chassis and Ford's lightweight V-8. The project was originally conceived around Chevy's race-proven small-block, but when GM refused to play ball Shelby successfully wooed Ford in its place. No doubt the General would soon regret its decision; once an experimental hi-po 260 V-8 from Ford was bolted into AC's specially reinforced chassis, the potential of this new creation was obvious. The "Cobra" worked well right out of the box; more important, it ran rings around the heavier Corvette.

A small run of street-legal Cobras arrived in 1962, just in time to launch a simultaneous racing legend. The first few cars barely had time to heat up their tires before Shelby's team and others began taking them to the track, and in most cases not even the thoroughbred GTs from Italy could catch the lightweight Fords. Well into the 1960s, Shelby's Cobra Sports Roadsters and streamlined Cobra Daytona Coupes regularly embarrassed all comers. Cobras packing 289-inch small-blocks captured SCCA titles and even, in 1965, the prestigious FIA World Manufacturer's Championship. For 1965 Shelby dropped the 289 Cobra in favor of one with a 427-inch big-block under the hood. Though still clothed in classic Cobra bodywork, these bruisers were virtually all new under the skin, and while the 427 never matched the 289's record on the track, it was one of the most potent cars of all time. This heritage, combined with ultra-low production (just 655 small-blocks and 348 big-blocks in all) guarantees the Cobra's collectability. More common but no less interesting were the Mustang-based Shelbys, sold from 1965 to 1970.

Ford's competition record in the 1960s is a fitting testimonial to what can be accomplished when one talented automotive company puts its skills—and its pocketbook—into racing.

3

General Motors Corporation

As the 1950s began, GM placed four cars in the top ten in model year sales; as the decade ended, the number had grown to five when Cadillac crept into the last spot. In between, the General produced some of the most memorable cars of a very memorable automotive decade.

The '55, '56, and '57 Chevys achieved stellar sales, and became latter day 1950s icons, as did the flamboyant fins of the 1959 Cadillac. A future American superstar got off to a rocky start in the form of the 1953 Corvette. The fiberglass flyer took several years to catch fire, but by the late 1950s "America's only sports car" was starting to live up to its early promise.

The 265-cubic inch, small-block Chevy engine appeared in 1955, putting the heat in Chevy's "Hot Ones" lineup, and started a lineage of motors that put the heart in the Heartbeat of America lineup for decades to follow.

Oldsmobiles' Rocket 88 overhead valve V-8 was one year old in 1950, and it dominated the racetracks of the day. It also gave a trickle-down boost to the entire Olds lineup.

Speaking of image boosters, a trio of GM cars arrived in 1953 in time to buff up the status of Buick, Oldsmobile, and Cadillac, with the addition of the Skylark, Fiesta, and Eldorado, respectively. These pricey, limited-build convertibles were dazzling, but short-lived, because only Eldorado survived past 1955.

Buick, Pontiac, and Olds ranked four, five, and six in model year sales in 1950. By 1959, those three slots were occupied by Pontiac, Olds, and Rambler, which nudged ahead of slumping, seventh place Buick on the strength of a roaring market for compact cars.

The 1960s were punctuated by several noteworthy cars culled from the General's ranks. Three

Coming off its best-ever sales year in 1963, Cadillac was on a roll in 1964. Styling for the flagship ragtop was a gentle evolution, with legitimate tail fins making their 17th (and last) annual appearance.

Cadillac's 1959 styling epitomized all that was good and bad about 1950s auto design. For sheer outrageousness its grille, fins, and greenhouse would be pretty hard to beat, but even GM Styling feared it had finally gone too far. For 1960, all of GM's models began a retreat into progressively more tasteful, balanced, and sophisticated styling. Caddy sales showed it was the right decision, marking a steady progression from 142,184 units in 1960 to 223,237 for 1969.

This Firebird displays a classic pony car interior—buckets and console up front, smallish occasional seating in back. The driver's view includes a hood-mounted tach, which was introduced by Pontiac in 1967 and went on to be a highly desired option.

generations of Corvette were around for at least part of this decade, including the 1963–67 cars that are generally regarded as the best 'Vette generation yet. Corvair was Chevy's first compact—

The Firebird did double duty for Pontiac. Perfectly suited for the pony car market that was flourishing in 1967, its huge option sheet also let buyers fit it out as a muscle-car if they liked. Witness this stunning 1967 400-cubic-inch-displacement convertible: A Firebird so equipped could turn 0–60 times in the mid-sixes, a figure that still holds up 30-plus years later.

the radical, rear engine design offered an interesting counterpoint to the many more conventional offerings that it competed with in the 1960s. Pontiac Firebird and Chevy Camaro were late arrivals to the pony car party that Mustang was throwing, but they proved to be worthy adversaries and durable to boot. Thirty plus years after their introduction, you can still order one at your local dealer. Two other long-playing name plates were also 1960s stalwarts—the Chevy Impala and Pontiac Grand Prix. Impala provided a full menu of full size models while Grand Prix came just one way—hardtop coupes with a sporting disposition. Finally, GM was in the thick of it in the power wars, with practically every model in every lineup eventually offered with high performance options—or at least a sportier look.

Chevy Camaro/Pontiac Firebird
Two for the Road

By the time GM's top sport coupes—the Camaro and Firebird—were out of the gate in the 1960s pony car stakes, Ford's Mustang was already well down the

For as long as there have been cars, people have taken stock versions and tried to improve them. In the wild and woolly 1960s—when the factory's own performance cars were none too shabby themselves—Chevy dealer/racer Don Yenko offered his tire-shredding Yenko Camaro powered by a built version of the 427 Chevy V-8. It is thought that just 64 examples were made in 1968, including this one.

track. Despite this, the General's joint entries went on to shine as two of the most memorable cars of the decade. They were so good, in fact, that they continue to succeed even as they pass 30—long after many of their contemporaries have since gone to pasture.

If GM management needed any convincing about the viability of personal sporty cars, the Mustang would push them over the edge. Once Ford's phenomenal success was seen everyone else scrambled to field his or her own version of the pony car. Certainly the most successful were GM's corporate siblings, the Chevy Camaro and Pontiac Firebird.

In the early 1960s, Chevy found that a sporty version of its Corvair, the Monza, outsold the base car by a wide margin. But even this car was no match for the Mustang, and GM was suddenly in a race for a response. The true Mustang fighters were the Chevy Camaro and Pontiac Firebird twins, both launched in 1967. In the meantime, the 1964 Chevy II served as, to borrow a baseball term, the middle reliever, holding the runs down until the closer came in to finish the job.

The Camaro and Firebird's success was due in large measure to a faithful following of the Mustang recipe: one part style, one part price, add options to taste. It sounds simple, but it wasn't—as evidenced by the numerous half-baked pretenders that hit the market post-Mustang. GM's entries, however, were the real deal: well executed, beautifully styled cars that sold well from the start.

Known jointly as the F-cars (their internal GM designation), the first versions of the Camaro and Firebird featured classic pony car proportions and GM's usual deft 1960s detailing. The Firebird's main distinguishing mark was its distinctive family nose, a chromium beak sitting proudly front and center in the grille.

The Bonneville Convertible for 1960

Pontiac becomes you wherever its Wide-Track takes you

In the lush of evening, head for some place special…in a Pontiac. The eagerness of this inspiring automobile will captivate you completely. On curves and turns you'll feel the forthright control and upright stability that come from Wide-Track Wheels. As you go, a fascinating quietness will stimulate your conversation and relax your ride. When you arrive, bask for a moment in the respectful spotlight of admiration that's always focused on this striking, tasteful car. It's all part of owning a Pontiac. Plan to make a personal appearance in a Pontiac soon. See your Pontiac dealer and see how easy it is to call one your own.

PONTIAC THE ONLY CAR WITH WIDE-TRACK WHEELS

Pontiac spawned some of the most artistic print ads of the 1960s. To stretch a point about the benefits of the Wide-Track concept, the illustrator has drawn a 1960 Bonneville convertible with heroically broad proportions—about what you'd see if you dropped a very large anvil on one.

Sharp-eyed viewers could tell a 1968 F-car from a 1967 by the federally mandated side marker lights and the disappearance of the vent windows. The 1969s were even easier to spot: Though largely unchanged below the skin, the Camaro took on prominent fender creases and a wide egg-crate grille, while the Firebird's nose was bobbed with body-color housings around the headlights. Both 1969s were more angular and less voluptuous than before, and their wheel openings were cut almost square.

Of particular interest to collectors were the Camaro Indy Pace Car replicas of 1969. This was the second time that a Camaro had paced the 500 in its young life (also in 1967), but the first time Chevy capitalized on it by selling replicas in quantity. Nearly 3,500 buyers ponied up the requisite $3,500 to take one home.

Also notable were the F-car's high-performance variants. A mechanical smorgasbord of engines was available from the start, accompanied by optional upgrades for the suspension and brakes. Excellent performers and drivers in their day, these cars remain perennial favorites among latter-day car buffs. The two most famous performance off-shoots—the Camaro Z-28 and Firebird Trans-Am—owed their existence to GM's interest in boosting brand prestige through racing. Competing in the SCCA Trans-Am class at the time required manufacturers to produce "streetable" copies for the public, so Chevy created 602 Z-28s in 1967 to homologate the car's stiffer underpinnings and high-winding 302-inch V-8. The Firebird Trans-Am didn't join its cousin until 1969 and, ironically enough, Pontiac never pursued the SCCA Trans-Am class with anything like Chevy's vigor, even though its star pony car co-opted the name.

Cleverly engineered, reasonably priced, and nicely appointed, the Camaro and Firebird proved durable as well as desirable. In second-generation form they survived the sleepy 1970s with the same Ferrari-like shape that appeared at the start of the decade, and re-emerged in the techno-laden 1980s with sheer-look styling and an option list long enough to spec the car out from a cushy cruiser to cut-throat racer. Approaching the end of the 1990s, there are still occasional rumblings about killing off these rear-wheel-drive pony cars, but as long as there are whole new generations to discover what all the shouting was about in the 1960s, the F-cars are likely to live on.

38

Chevy Corvair
Backward Glance at the Future

In the 1960s, the Big Three tried to think small. Earlier, the independents and Volkswagen had the compact class largely to themselves. That all changed in 1960 with the advent of compact competitors from all the major manufacturers. Chevy's entry into the small-car fracas was easily the most radical. Powered by an air-cooled, horizontally opposed, six-cylinder rear engine like the fours of VW and Porsche, the Corvair was a different animal for Detroit and an interesting alternative for Americans.

Among the small herd of compact cars that appeared in the early 1960s, the Corvair was unique—even *radical*. The first hint of how different the Corvair was could be found as soon as you opened the deck; where most Americans were used to putting their luggage, instead they found an air-cooled flat-six. Displacing 140 cubic inches at the start, the engine was rather complex and heavier than its designers had wanted. This rear weight bias and an underdeveloped rear suspension contributed to oversteer in the first-generation cars, a potentially dangerous problem made worse by the Corvair's sensitivity to tire pressure. Consumer advocate Ralph Nader later indicted Detroit—and specifically the Corvair—in his 1965 book *Unsafe at any Speed*. While many of the problems Nader cited had been solved before the book was even published, the Corvair's reputation never recovered.

Chevy added a midyear wrinkle to its fledgling subcompact in 1960 with the addition of the Monza versions. Boasting bucket seats and up-level trim, the Monza was an early salvo into the personal-sports market and helped jump-start Corvair sales after a slow debut. A second-generation

Corvair appeared for 1965 with clean styling and a redesigned suspension for much improved handling. Aside from the Corvette, the Corvair was Detroit's first production car with fully independent suspension.

The Corvair's unconventional engine wasn't too conducive to traditional hop-up techniques, so Chevrolet added optional turbocharging late in the 1962 model year. Designated as Monza Spyders, these fleet little cars packed 70 more horses than standard (150 versus 80). Turbocharged Corvairs continued being built into the second generation, where the hotter cars were called Corsas rather than Monzas.

The Corvair's life spanned the 1960s exactly, and its failure to live longer had more to do with horses than handling. The introduction of the Mustang in 1964 and the Camaro and Firebird in 1967 took away its sporty-car buyers, while down-market versions of traditional cars could compete with it for the economy-minded.

An air-cooled rear engine made the Corvair the least conventional compact on the market when it appeared in 1960—and it remained that way for 1965, when the second generation appeared. Sporty Monza models (like this 1964) perked up the nameplate's image and tried to hold Chevy's place against the stampeding Mustang until the Camaro and Firebird arrived in 1967.

Special Forces

The General's High-Performance Troops

Camaro. Corvette. Firebird. Gran Sport. GTO. 4-4-2. The roll-call of GM performance cars of the 1960s is enough to make grown people salivate. These were the front-line names, the most fearsome of the General's army. But, in the "Have it Your Way" 1960s, just about every GM class from subcompact to full-size could be optioned out with an arsenal of go-fast (or at least look-fast) weaponry.

As mentioned earlier, the Corvette, Camaro, and Firebird were among the most noteworthy performers in GM's lineup. In the 1960s, the Corvette continued its evolution with stunning styling and progressive mechanical refinement. As for the pony

The GTO started life in 1964 as an option package on the intermediate Pontiac Tempest, then went on to become one of the premier musclecars of the era. GTOs from 1965 (like this Tri-Power) are especially prized today, combining clean, strong styling with some very potent powerplants. The Tri-Power option bumped horsepower from 335 to 360 at a cost of $116.

cars, snarly, small-block-powered specialty models competed on the track and spun off streetable versions for the road. And while they were initially offered with a base-model six, most Camaros and Firebirds rumbled off the lot with an optional small or big-block under their hoods.

Long before the F-cars, however, Detroit had already hit on the idea of stuffing big-car engines into intermediate-sized bodies. In so doing, they defined the musclecar.

Though 1950s cars such as the Chrysler 300 followed a similar formula, the first self-proclaimed musclecar was Pontiac's GTO. While the *Gran Turismo Omologato* handle was unselfconsciously borrowed from the Italians, this was a distinctly American creation. Initially, the GTO was an option package on the Tempest Le Mans: A 389-inch V-8 with

Once Pontiac's GTO proved successful, other GM divisions wanted a piece of the action. Oldsmobile's entry was dubbed the 4-4-2 (a rather strained symbol for four-barrel carburetor, four-speed transmission, and two exhausts). The 4-4-2 was Oldsmobiles' 1960s muscle standard bearer—and a link with the division's almost forgotten 1950s performance heritage.

As the GTO was to the Tempest and the 4-4-2 was to the Cutlass, so the Gran Sport was to Buick's Skylark. An option package when it debuted in 1965, the Gran Sport boasted a 401-inch Buick "Nailhead" V-8 rated at 325 brake horsepower and a massive 445 pound-feet of torque. With corporate modesty typical of the era, Buick ads called the Gran Sport "a howitzer with windshield wipers."

The Bonneville and the rest of Pontiac's full-sized lineup rode into 1963 on fresh styling. The Bonneville name was first applied to a Pontiac in 1957 when it was used on a fuel-injected, semi-custom convertible with a very high price ($5,782) and very low build (630 produced). Like several other Pontiacs of the 1960s (Firebird, Grand Prix) the name remains in Pontiac's lineup to this day.

325 to 348 brake horsepower was the foundation of the package, supplemented by a three-speed manual, beefed-up suspension, fatter tires, faster steering, dual exhausts, and identifying trim. Best of all, the GTO could run 0 to 60 in the midsixes and the quarter-mile in the 14s. Buyer response was brisk: More than 32,000 were sold the first year, dwarfing Pontiac's predicted total of 5,000. A star was born.

The success of the "Goat" prompted GM to share the wealth (internally, that is), so when the GTO returned for 1965—now promoted from an option package to a full model—it was joined by

The original (and current) owner of this 1965 Olds 88 Dynamic convertible couldn't find any standard colors to his liking, but in those days GM would let you special-order any GM color you wished. For the princely sum of $49, he got to wrap this ragtop in a coat of Rally Red.

Buick's Skylark Gran Sport, Chevy's Chevelle SS-396, and the Oldsmobile 4-4-2.

This foursome of new muscle stars shined for the rest of the decade, sharing the same basic chassis and similar bodies throughout. The straight-shouldered styling of the 1965 models gave way to long, tapered lines in 1966 and 1967. That, in turn, yielded to a tidy-looking shape on a 112-inch wheelbase that carried GM's intermediate musclecars through the end of the decade.

44

Chevy Corvette
Glass Windows

After a shaky start, the Corvette found its footing late in the 1950s and has never looked back. During the 1960s it saw three body types, two chassis, countless engine options, and a glorious five-year span that many now consider its best ever: 1963 to 1967.

Of the three styling generations seen on Corvettes in the 1960s, the last one—1968 and later—was the most controversial. It would also prove the most durable, carrying the car through 1982. The swoopy design, descended from GM's Mako Shark II show car, was bigger outside and smaller inside than the 1963–1967 style it replaced, and Chevy was still working out the kinks when production began in 1968. No less than four 427 options were offered in 1969, the most popular being the 390-horse version as fit to this Daytona Yellow convertible.

Corvette bodies went through three distinct designs in the 1960s. The final year of the first-generation ("C1") Corvette came in 1962. These were the last Corvettes to have an external trunk lid, the last with a solid rear axle, and the last with exposed headlights. They looked and felt like direct descendants of the original 1950s sports car.

But their replacement was something else entirely. The 1963 to 1967 models—now known as Sting Rays, "midyear," or C2 cars—brought plenty of performance enhancements and a gorgeous new body. *Two* bodies, actually, for the first Corvette coupe arrived at the same time. The 1963 Corvette's all-new chassis sported independent rear suspension, and air conditioning became available for those who didn't think the cars were cool enough as is. Four-wheel disc brakes became standard equipment in 1965, and the same year saw the final season of the fuel-injected small-block (until 1982). Now big-block V-8s were to carry the performance ball, initially as a 425-horse 396. Style-wise, the cars tended to get even cleaner through the midyears, progressively using less fakery and frivolous trim on their taut, Bill Mitchell-designed bodies.

The next major change came in 1968. The thoroughly redesigned body sported swoopy, dramatic styling over an essentially unchanged chassis, but the cars weren't received well at first. This was due not only to the strength of the preceding design but also to the new car's indifferent build quality, bigger size and weight, and some unfortunate problems with interior and mechanical packaging.

True to the Corvette's nature, as the C3 evolved many of its original weaknesses were systematically overcome. In the end, the classic, Coke-bottle shape proved good enough to stick around largely unchanged through 1982.

Front-wheel drive wasn't a new concept in the 1960s, but it was still unusual—particularly on a car as big as an Oldsmobile. Not since the FWD Cords of the late twenties and thirties had an American manufacturer tried anything like it. The Olds Toronado debuted in 1966, followed by the internally similar Cadillac Eldorado in 1967. Both cars featured graceful styling and innovative engineering, though understeer and driveline reliability would be ongoing problems. Under the Olds' dramatic sheet metal was a 119-inch wheelbase, a 425-cubic-inch-displacement Rocket V-8, and a unique two-piece Turbo Hydra-Matic transmission originally conceived for a Corvette concept car. The new Olds sold well at first, and while the numbers dropped off later, it survived to establish a name for itself. Oldsmobile's stylish Toro remained in the lineup through 1992.

This Roman Red ragtop combines two Chevrolet classics of the 1960s: the Impala and 409. The Impala became the company's best-selling line in the 1960s and looks particularly dashing in this 1962 convertible form. Under the hood was an engine so good that the Beach Boys immortalized it in song.

Chevy Impala

Meet Chevy's John Doe

Chevy had plenty of interesting products in the 1960s—the unorthodox Corvair, the sporty Corvette, and the fashionable workhorse El Camino, to name a few. But none was more important to the company than the Impala, the full-sized heart and soul of the Bowtie lineup. The other models kept Chevy's profile high in their respective markets, but the Impala's success as a mainstream seller kept Chevy at or near the top of the charts, allowing the company the luxury of taking chances elsewhere.

The Impala was one of Chevy's big breadwinners throughout the 1960s. The full-sized offering closed out the decade with its formal lines stretched over a 119-inch wheelbase, as shown on this 1969. Impalas were offered in no less than 10 separate models that year, and more than 777,000 were built.

The name Impala is so synonymous with Chevy in the 1960s that you'd assume the marque had been in the lineup for decades. Not so. The first Chevy to carry the name appeared in 1958 as a top-line spin-off of the Bel Air series. Early success ushered the Impala to full-series status for 1959, one rung up from the Bel Air.

Chevy opened the 1960s in the second year of a wild styling cycle. The bizarre, batwing look of the full-sized 1959 Chevys had been toned down for 1960, but it was still a long way from sedate. Chevy followed up the extroverted shape of 1960 with balanced, pencil-box lines in 1961–1964—arguably the most classic design ever to carry the Impala name. Mid-decade models of 1965 and 1966 offered a handsome, slightly heavier and more formal look, which was followed in turn by ever longer and larger cars for the balance of the decade.

Two Impalas of the 1960s deserve special attention. Super Sport was the name Chevy gave to the swiftest of its models, and at various times in the decade the Impala SS was either an option or

The Grand Prix celebrated its second year in the Pontiac lineup in 1963 with crisp new styling. These strong and sporting GPs were popular: Just under 73,000 were produced in 1963, more than twice as many as 1962.

a subseries. Either way, the SS basics were a combination of show-and-go items such as special trim, spinner-style hubcaps, whitewall tires, beefed-up brakes and suspension, tachometer, and power steering and brakes. Of course, there was plenty of under-hood firepower to back up the emblems. The first engine of note was a 348-inch V-8, but the

348's claim to fame has less to do with its own performance than with being the father of the fabled 409—one of several legendary engines powering Chevys in the 1960s. For most of the 1960s, Chevy took the SS package in two directions simultaneously: strictly cosmetic or strictly business. The initials graced everything from straight-six cars to hair-raising big-blocks. Perhaps the most commonly seen (and most desirable) were those packing the highly acclaimed 327 small-block.

Another 1960s Impala of note was the Caprice. This high-end entry was introduced in mid-1965 as an option package in response to Ford's upwardly mobile LTD. Graduating to full-model status in 1966, the Caprice was the King of Chevys back when Chevy was the Crown Prince of GM. The Caprice was essentially a dressy Impala sporting some of the luxury features that buyers traditionally sought elsewhere from GM. The first versions offered a vinyl top, blacked-out grille, special trim and wheel covers, and a cushy interior with *faux*-wood appointments.

Whether the Caprice's move upscale caused any defections from one GM camp to another is uncertain, but its effect on Chevy's bottom line was unmistakable. The Caprice sold well over 100,000 units annually through the end of the 1960s.

The Impala and Caprice remained mainstays of Chevy's lineup through the 1970s, when both reverted to subseries status. The Impala dropped off the map as a model designation after 1985, only to reappear again in 1994 as a special high-performance model in the Caprice series. The Impala SS cars of 1994 to 1996 are certain entries on any list of future collectibles.

Pontiac Grand Prix
Wide Trackin' with Style

Though often hard to define, each GM division has always had a slightly different market orientation. In the 1960s, Pontiac's emphasis was on luxury with performance. No car captured that approach better than the Grand Prix.

Despite offering just one body style, the Grand Prix was a steady seller in Pontiac's full-sized lineup throughout the 1960s. These hardtop coupes didn't invent the personal-luxury category, but they did provide a stylish, less expensive alternative to the pioneering four-seater Thunderbird.

The Grand Prix gained size throughout the decade, keeping pace with the Catalina-based models it shared its platform with. The trend was reversed in 1969, with the introduction of an intermediate-sized GP. The first models were powered

The 1969 Grand Prix was a half-foot shorter and 4 inches narrower than the 1968 it replaced. The dramatic new exterior was balanced with a wraparound dash inside, a nod to aviation design. This fine 1969 features a 390-horse 428 V-8.

by Pontiac's 389 V-8, which was replaced in 1967 by the 400. Consistent with the times, performance options were available for any GP buyer who wanted more power with luxury.

In terms of styling, the crisp, formal-looking 1963–1964 was a watershed in American design. The 1967-only convertible was another hands-down winner, looking rather menacing with its hideaway headlights and battering-ram beak. And at the end of the decade, the smart-looking, downsized 1969 GP arrived, riding for the first time on its own chassis with a 118-inch wheelbase.

The Grand Prix is another 1960s nameplate that's proved to have staying power. The strictly two-door concept was abandoned in 1990 with the addition of a four-door sedan. Today, the Grand Prix continues to serve as Pontiac's intermediate standard bearer.

4

Chrysler Corporation

Like GM, Chrysler's engineering accomplishments in the 1950s paved the way for some of Chrysler's more memorable cars in the 1960s. Chrysler's hemispherical head V-8 engine started appearing under hoods throughout the lineup early in the decade and would develop into one of the most fearsome musclecar motors that the 1960s would ever see. The year 1957 was particularly good: Virgil Exner's design work hit a high watermark, and the introduction of torsion-bar suspension gave Chrysler products the industry edge in handling as well.

The decade saw the emergence of several soon-to-be coveted cars such as Chrysler's 300 (arriving in 1955), Plymouth's Fury (new in '56) and Dodges equipped with the hot D500 package. Even DeSoto chipped in a blue chip 1950s car with its Adventurer, though the marque would last only through 1961.

Mopar offerings in the 1960s were varied and colorful—sometimes quite literally, as many models began offering eye popping paint choices late in the decade. Notable Chrysler products of the period ranged from the full-size staple Furys to the trusty and popular compact duo of Plymouth Barracuda and Dodge Dart. The Imperial took the high road and sought to lure luxury car buyers away from Lincoln and Cadillac. Meanwhile, on the roads measured in quarter-mile strips and wide-banked ovals, a variety of Chrysler products distinguished themselves. Two Pentastar-produced mills—the 426 hemi and the 440 Magnum—would write very long chapters in the annals of 1960s performance cars. Two variants of the swoopy Dodge Charger (Charger 500 and Charger Daytona) were turned loose on NASCAR

The GTX was Plymouth's high-line hot rod, combining performance hardware with upgraded interior and comfort features. Though the engines were both heavy big blocks (standard 440 Magnum or optional 426 Hemi), a beefed-up chassis gave the car cornering abilities on par with most anything in its class. *Car Life* called it "... one of the best handling sedan chassis we have ever driven."

Imperial convertibles were never high-volume cars. Production of the 1964 to 1968 ragtops ranged from a high of 922 (1964) to a low of 474 (1968). A 1968 Crown convertible like this one had a sticker price of $6,522. Tipping the scales at an incredible 4,845 pounds, the Imperial drew power from a 350-horsepower, 440-inch V-8.

tracks, and both models spun off street versions for sale to the public. The 300 series continued to ply its "part gentleman, part brawler" persona before sliding back into the mainstream Chrysler lineup by decade's end. Finally, one can't write about Chrysler products of the 1960s without a good fish story. Barracuda began life as a sporty alternative to Chevy's Corvair before being drafted for the altogether different role of Mustang fighter. Once this role confusion was sorted out, the Barracuda turned into one of the finest pony cars of the era.

Chrysler Imperial
Lincolnesque Royalty

There's a more-than-passing resemblance between the classic Imperials of the mid-1960s and the Lincoln Continentals of the same period. The angular elegance of the 1964-1968 Imperials seems parallel to the Lincoln's straight-edge styling, and for good reason—the Imperial's lead designer was Elwood Engel, key man on the team that created the 1961 Continental.

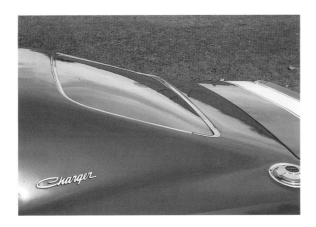

Arriving at Chrysler in 1961, Elwood Engel replaced Virgil Exner, the man who'd directed every Imperial design since the cars achieved separate-marque status in 1955. Engel had been one of seven stylists responsible for the classic Lincoln Continentals of 1961–1967, and those cars' influence was translated to the Imperials by their new design chief.

The first Imperial to show Engel's full imprint was the 1964. The new car's flat, horizontal bodyline replaced years of flying fins and tacked-on trim, and the result was a massive sales jump (23,285 units from 14,108). Not surprisingly, there was little incentive after that to mess with a good thing, so the Imperial was allowed to age gracefully through 1966, with changes generally limited to yearly face-lifts. In 1965, the front end got headlamps under glass and a new 440-inch V-8 for a net gain of 10 horsepower.

The 1967–1968 Imperials evolved a bit more, with a slightly more tapered but still-formal look. Under the skin there were major structural changes for 1967, however, as the car abandoned its body-on-frame approach for full unibody construction. Starting in 1969, the Imperial marque was re-absorbed into Chrysler's lineup. This was also the debut year for Chrysler's "Fuselage Styling," a look that was either bulbous or beefy, depending on your taste.

The Imperial remained at the head of Chrysler's

A flush grille and rear glass made the Charger 500 slipperier than its brethren, and hence more competitive on the NASCAR circuit. The limited run of street versions offered standard 440 or optional Hemi power. While the Charger 500 was effective, it was left to the radical shovel-nosed, high-winged Dodge Charger Daytona and Plymouth Road Runner Superbird to bring the stock-car title to Chrysler. NASCAR banned the winged cars shortly thereafter.

Dodge's Charger had existed for two years when this fresh restyle appeared in 1968. Still riding on Chrysler's B-body platform, the tasteful new lines made people forget about the ungainly fastbacks of 1966 and 1967. Most of the Charger's sheet metal was basic Coronet, but Dodge's stylists deftly hid this. The Charger's R/T option was carried over from 1967 and packed a collection of hardware befitting its "Road/Track" handle. Starting with a 440 Magnum or optional Hemi, R/T Chargers also boasted beefier suspension, upgraded interior, and a loud set of bumblebee stripes. The 1968 Charger was a hit: Its production of 96,000-plus units was nearly twice that of the 1966 and 1967 cars combined. Styling updates in 1969 and 1970 kept the great shape popular—but made the inelegant post-1971 Chargers look even more unfortunate in comparison.

lineup through 1975, when it was discontinued. The name was revived for a stylish, bustle-backed sedan Chrysler produced from 1981 to 1983, and it resurfaced once more in 1990 for a one-year run of New Yorker-based front-wheel-drive luxury sedans.

Try though they did, the 1960s Imperials never quite reached the ranks of automotive royalty. Probably the biggest factor working against them was the strength of the competition, Lincoln in particular, setting a very high standard in the 1960s. Though the 1964-1969 Imperials boasted fine lines and an unparalleled ride, their build quality was a clear notch below the competition's in this unforgivingly demanding niche.

Dodge Charger 500/Charger Daytona

The Charger was a midsized staple of the Dodge lineup in the late 1960s. The first-generation cars (1966-1967) were large fastbacks, a style that had a curious burst of popularity in the mid-1960s. Though still much the same under the skin, the post-1968 models were amazingly different looking: swoopy, aggressive—and popular. There were as many restyled 1968s sold as in the previous two years combined.

When manufacturers go racing, sanctioning bodies often require them to produce limited quantities of a given model for sale to the public. As thinly veiled race cars, many such "homologation specials" have become road-going mega-stars.

Dodge built not just one, but two such cars in 1969, both bearing the Charger name. The Charger 500 was the first, and while a handful went out to do battle on NASCAR's ovals, a limited number was also made for the street. (Five hundred were supposed to be built to satisfy NASCAR, but only 392 were made in the end.) The Charger 500's changes were mostly made in the interest of better aerodynamics. Up front, the standard car's hidden headlights were done away with and the grille was pulled forward to be flush with the front of the car. Also flush was the rear glass, replacing the standard recessed window. Special striping wrapped around

the tail and under the hood was a standard 440 Magnum or optional 426 Hemi. It was buyer's choice for transmission: four-speed or TorqueFlite.

Street versions delivered on their performance promises, and *Car Life* proclaimed the 500 its Supercar of the Year. In NASCAR, though, the Chargers still found themselves chasing Talladegas and Cyclones around the circuit. Thus, in the middle of the model year, Chrysler upped the ante and launched its first winged warrior, the Dodge Charger Daytona. Radically styled to push the aerodynamics envelope, the Daytona—followed in 1970 by the similar Plymouth Road Runner Superbird—featured tapered steel snouts and a tall aluminum wing. Towering 2 feet over the rear deck, these wings produced an adjustable stabilizing down force on the race cars and irresistible, ticket-me first looks on the production models. The 440 Magnum was again

In the best letter-car tradition, the 1960 Chrysler 300F was equal parts gentleman and street brawler. Four-place buckets made their 300 debut in 1960 (the driver's seat swiveled for easy ingress and egress), and its 413-inch Ram-induction V-8 was a formidable performer. Chrysler 300s kicked sand in the competition's face at Daytona Beach in 1960, covering the flying mile at just under 145 miles per hour. A scant 248 300F convertibles like this one were built that year.

standard, the Hemi once more optional. About 505 were built for street sale, all of which were finished at Creative Industries, a Detroit specialty shop.

Introduced in NASCAR late in the 1969 season, the Daytona made an immediate impact with two wins in four starts. The following year they romped and stomped their way to wins in roughly three quarters of the races they entered. And then, almost as quickly as they arrived, the winged cars were chased from the circuit in punishment for their success. A rules change banished the big Mopars from NASCAR and ushered them into the history books.

Maybe the "L" in 300L stood for Last, as 1965 was the final year of letter-car status for Chrysler's elegant brutes. With the 300 pendulum swinging away from performance and back toward luxury, the 300L managed a healthy blend of both. Its 413-inch, 360-brake horsepower engine was tamer than that of some 300s of the past but surely no stone. Crisp 1965 styling drew influences from the Imperial and looked especially good as a convertible.

Chrysler 300

The Elegant Brutes

The 1950s 300-series "letter cars" were among the most respected automobiles ever built by the Chrysler Corporation. But the 1960s saw the 300s ride in near the top of their game and ride out just one step shy of extinction. To appreciate the 300's story, you need to step back into the 1950s and the roots of these elegant brutes.

Introduced in 1955, Chrysler's 300-C was the embodiment of the luxury performance car. Joining the Pentastar perennials Windsor and New Yorker, the new 300 was a sweet styling mishmash. Equal parts Imperial, Windsor, New Yorker, and parts bin, the powerful shape was nevertheless clean and potent. That look was no teaser, either—under the hood was a tweaked version of Chrysler's 331-inch Hemi rated at 300 horsepower, making it the most powerful production car in America.

The 300s were hard-driving, hard-riding cars, and their competition counterparts were hard chargers as well. In 1955, the 300 snapped up the first NASCAR race it entered, and the model went on to collect the NASCAR and AAA titles in its debut season.

For the rest of the 1950s, the 300 set an enviable standard. Entering the 1960s it was still a sobering performance car and would weather years of uneven Chrysler styling with as much grace as any model in the lineup. But as the decade progressed, Chrysler's performance philosophy shifted and the 300 was ushered gently back toward the mainstream. It was almost as if the company viewed performance as being somehow undignified for the veteran letter cars (300-C for 1955, 300-D for 1956, and so on). While Chrysler flexed its muscles elsewhere, the 300 gracefully coasted into a more unassuming role; 1965 was the last year of the let-

The dictionary defines *fuselage* as ". . . the central structure of an airplane," so it should surprise no one that Chrysler's 1969 "Fuselage Styling" resulted in cars that needed a 747 hangar for storage. In truth, the 1969 Mopars were longer, wider, and heavier than their predecessors—but not nearly so much as they looked. The brawny new theme worked well on the muscular Three Hundred. The exclusive letter series was abandoned after 1965, and in 1969 the name was spelled out, rather than denoted numerically. The model could be optioned with a 375-horse "TNT" version of Chrysler's work-horse 440 V-8.

ter cars and the last time the 300 would be a true limited-production machine. By decontenting (some would say *neutering*) the 300s, Chrysler could sell them for less; and since the fast-car market was being covered elsewhere in the lineup, the company let the 300 float toward more luxury, less exclusivity, and higher volume. Though this watered down

The first-generation Barracuda fished both sides of the stream, offering everything from a frugal slant-six in the base car to a powerful 383-cubic-inch-displacement V-8 in "glassback," notchback, or convertible form.

its once-proud reputation, it's doubtful that the company lost much sleep over it. The more mainstream 300s kept the cash register ringing.

The 300 became the "Three Hundred" in 1969, perhaps because Chrysler's wide, bulbous new styling theme gave enough room for spelling it all out. But however you spelled it, the model only hung around through 1971.

Plymouth Barracuda
Fish Story

Plymouth's Barracuda spent a lot of time swimming upstream. Designed to compete with sporty compacts, it was unceremoniously drafted for the pony car wars when the Mustang started setting sales records and riding roughshod on the market.

Pity the poor Barracuda. It had the sheer misfortune of being launched just two weeks before Ford's Mustang. Once the similarly sized Mustang began breaking every first-year record on the books, the new Plymouth compact gained a serious case of mistaken identity. The Valiant-based Barracuda was originally designed to compete as a sporty subcompact against cars like the Corvair Monza and Ford Falcon Sprint. But because of its similar size, sporty-ish looks, and almost identical birthday, the comparisons were made with the revolutionary new Mustang instead.

The first Barracudas featured a large, curved rear window and a fold-down back seat. Essentially just a Valiant under the skin, the Barracuda

Buyers were distinctly underwhelmed by Chrysler's downsized 1962 lineup, and all Mopars would get more traditional styling the next year. But racers liked the smaller, lighter 1962s, and they practically sprained their smiles when a bigger big block was made optional in 1963. Chrysler's big wedge-head V-8 was bored out from 413- to 426-cubic inch displacement that year and offered 370 or 415 brake horsepower, depending on induction. Pavement physics suggested that a downsized car plus an upsized engine should equal plenty of molten rubber, and indeed it did. Cars packing the 426 Super Stock engine, like this Savoy, were the dominant draggers of their day.

was economical, cute, inexpensive, and utilitarian. Where it came up short (relative to Mustang) was in the looks and fun departments. More than 100,000 Barracudas were sold in 1965-1966, which would seem like pretty good numbers if Mustang hadn't had such runaway success.

The second-generation cars of 1967 to 1969 were much improved, and this is where the Barracuda finally found itself. Now firmly down the pony car path, the Barracuda was available as a ragtop, a quirky notchback, and a fastback. Engine-wise, Chrysler's bulletproof slant-six was still standard, but small-block V-8s, and even a 426 Hemi or 440 Wedge, could be ordered. A Barracuda from this period optioned with, say, the stiff Formula S suspension and a 340-inch V-8 could acquit itself admirably in both the quarter-mile and sports-car realms.

The Barracuda evolved again in 1970, the last major revamp the model saw through its final year in 1974. Included in the third and final generation was one particularly noteworthy muscle-car aberration—the AAR 'Cuda. The AAR's incredible balance of straight-line speed and predictable cornering made it quite possibly the best all-around performer of any musclecar ever built.

One of the 1964 Sport Fury's most interesting elements was its pagoda-style roofline. Also worth noting were the powertrains: 426 Street Wedge and Max Wedge engines were available to anyone who wanted to add sound to their Fury.

Plymouth Fury

Plymouth's 1960s Stalwart

Fury's progression in the Plymouth lineup made interesting watching. Launched as an exclusive, high-profile sport coupe in the 1950s, it settled down in the 1960s to be a middle-class mainstay for family transportation.

Having a great name doesn't guarantee success in a car any more than it does in a human, but you've got to admit that *Fury* is a fine handle. The Fury blew into town in midyear 1956 and estab-

lished itself at the top of the Plymouth lineup. Available only as a hardtop coupe in ivory with gold-anodized trim, it was clearly built to be noticed—and packing a 303-inch, 240-horse V-8, it gave the Plymouth's whole performance image a boost.

In the last year of the decade, Plymouth pulled the Fury back into the fold. Instead of the flashy standout it became the top-line series, and four-door models were added. An off-shoot subseries known as Sport Fury also appeared, with hardtop and convertible variants.

And so it was that Plymouth's soon-to-be stalwart entered the 1960s. The decade's first couple of

years weren't kind to Plymouth in general. Though blessed with fine torsion-bar handling and tight unibody construction, they were also saddled with ungainly styling and a ferocious propensity to rust. Sales slumped.

And then there was 1962, the year that Chrysler Corporation answered a question nobody asked. With the proven popularity of compact cars, Chrysler thought it saw a trend forming and started applying downsized styling to its whole lineup. The result was 1962's new, smaller, "standard" cars. As it turned out, buyers liked their compacts compact, but still wanted their big cars big. (Chrysler's gambit was a case of too little too soon; the rest of the industry didn't embark on a serious slim-down until rising fuel costs held a gun to their heads a decade later.) In the meantime, full-sized Fords and Chevys snapped up the alienated Mopar buyers and Plymouth sales took a free fall, landing in eighth place.

Even the midyear revival of the Sport Fury did little to move the company out of its corporate funk.

But if the smaller, standard-sized Chryslers didn't measure up for regular buyers, they suited the performance crowd just fine. With less weight to pull around and an ever-increasing arsenal of horsepower at its disposal, the Fury recaptured some of its early performance heritage. Plymouth pulled off an amazing 1-2-3 sweep in 1964 at NASCAR's big dance, the Daytona 500. Key to this stunning debut was the emergence of one of the legendary muscle motors of the 1960s—the 426 Hemi.

The next new Chrysler products appeared in 1965, when the Highland Park crew gave the public back what it wanted. The slab-sided "new-look" Furys now matched up size-wise with the competition (notably Ford's Galaxie and Chevy's Impala), and accounted for almost half of the 700,000-plus Plymouths sold in 1965. The Fury was now offered in so-called I, II, and III levels as well as a Sport Fury variant. The following year saw the addition of the high-line Fury VIP, launched to do battle with the Caprice and LTD.

On the downhill side of the decade, the Fury stayed big. For 1967 and 1968 it was reskinned again to look longer, thinner, and slightly less angular. Following tradition, these could be had with everything from the durable slant-six to the mighty 440 Wedge.

Fuselage styling was the theme for all Chrysler products in 1969, which meant more rotund body styles that were longer, wider, and heavier than before—though not nearly as heavy as they *looked*. But by this time sales of big cars like the Fury were off, and it was enough to cause the demise of the VIP after 1969. The Sport Fury continued through 1971, and the Fury name kept appearing sporadically through 1989, selling in ever-dwindling numbers as the market for full-sized RWDs shrank ever smaller. Ah, but what a ride it was: Starting in the late 1950s as Plymouth's young lion, the Fury roared through the 1960s as the company's top-line mainstream offering, then slowly retired and disappeared as an old gray sedan in the late 1980s.

Dodge Dart/Plymouth Valiant
Mainstream Mopar Compacts

The Dodge Dart and the Plymouth Valiant were two of the 1960s sales stars for Chrysler Corporation. They became close corporate cousins shortly into their lives and remained so until they disappeared in 1976; even so, at birth no one would have accused them of being related.

Option packaging has long been used to boost sales, and Dodge's White Hat Specials showed just how well that strategy could work. Here the package was largely cosmetic, though equally popular add-ons could include comfort features or performance hardware.

The 1960 Valiant was the first compact fielded by Chrysler. While at first a separate make, it became an official part of the Plymouth line a year later. Powered by a new, 170-inch slant-six (so called for its laid-over block, which allowed a lower hood), the Valiant had cheerful, quirky styling by Virgil Exner. The oddest of its many odd details was a bulge in the middle of the trunk made to look like the imprint of a spare tire—and known with occasional affection as the "toilet seat."

The Dodge Lancer joined Plymouth's Valiant in 1961, and together they did battle against the Ford Falcon, Mercury Comet, Chevy Corvair, Studebaker Lark, and the Rambler American. The Valiant's success handily bolstered Plymouth through several dry years in the early 1960s.

Dodge's Dart also made its debut in 1960, but at its inception it was a full-sized model built in three series and no less than 23 separate models. The Dart was an immediate smash, with more than 300,000 sold the first year—or a staggering 87 percent of Dodge's total 1960 production. But when the Valiant was restyled for 1963, a similar, longer-wheelbase Dodge version acquired the Dart name. From this point until the 1967 restyle, the Dart proved far more popular than the Lancer had ever been, while the Valiant continued posting strong sales. In keeping with market trends, both models spawned sporty versions with optional V-8s. A major restyle of the platform appeared in 1967, and from here on out through their final 1976 editions, the Valiant and Dart would be minor variations on this same theme.

A healthy 38,158 Satellites were made in 1966, of which 2,759 were ragtops. The restyled Belvedere/Satellite could be had with an optional Hemi under the hood, but probably just a handful of these wound up in Satellite convertibles like this one. Bought by an American working overseas, this example spent much of its early life across the pond. Imagine what must have gone through the mind of a Swiss driver about to be overtaken by this flying brick.

5

The Independents

The 1950s were a period of attrition for independent car makers. Several mergers were forged in an effort to stave off financial decline in an era of increasing competition. The death toll of those that did not survive the decade includes many names long familiar to American car buyers: Crosley, Hudson, Nash, Packard, Kaiser-Frazer, and Willys.

Nash and Hudson combined to form American Motors Corporation in 1954, but both names were history after 1957. Rambler and tiny Metropolitan were the sole standard bearers for AMC heading into the 1960s. Mini-car maker Crosley went out of production in 1952. Packard took over Studebaker in 1954 but vanished after 1958. Studebaker soldiered on through 1966. Kaiser-Frazer exited in 1955. Willys, bought by Kaiser-Frazer in 1954, dropped passenger car production after 1955 to concentrate on its Jeeps.

Despite this marketplace turbulence, some of the most interesting and significant automobiles to come out of the 1950s did so with an independent's name on their fenders. Cars such as the modernistic Kaiser-Darrin roadster, Studebaker's "Family Sports Car" Hawk models, Packard's elegant, early 1950s Caribbeans, the minicar Metropolitans, and Rambler's line of compacts—the first to demonstrate mass-market appeal—all would have been welcome additions to any of the Big Three's lineups.

The 1960s saw the ranks of the independents start with two and dwindle to just one, with the 1966 passing of Studebaker. The contributions of the smaller car builders in the decade were few but meaningful. Compact cars like Studebaker's Lark

While eye-popping colors were common by the end of the 1960s, AMC offered three particularly high-wattage hues as midyear options on the 1969 AMXs. Dubbed the "Big Bad AMXs," just 283 cars were built in this electrifying green. This one, owned by Victor and Barbara Nave, is even rarer still—it's a California 500 Edition, one of a series built to commemorate the AMX pace car of a 1969 Indy-car race at Ontario Motor Speedway.

Rushed into production in 1963, running improvements were made to the Avanti without slowing the production line or delineating between model years. This policy makes it hard to tell a 1963 from a 1964, but most (not all) 1964s sported distinctive squared-off headlight bezels. This one's a 1963.

and Rambler's American bolstered both of their respective manufacturers in the late 1950s and continued to do so until the Big Three caught up in the 1960s and cut into the small car market action in a big way.

The other lasting impression from the independents in the 1960s came in the performance realm. Studebaker's futuristic, fiberglass Avanti put a dazzling period on the end of the Studebaker story, while American Motors fielded surprisingly competitive musclecars in the latter part of the decade with names like Javelin, AMX, and SC/ Rambler.

Studebaker Avanti
Class in Fiberglass

By the early 1960s, Studebaker was a sinking ship. Yet in spite of its looming financial death and the resulting shoestring budgets, in its final years the South Bend, Indiana, company produced some of the finest cars in its history—a remarkable achievement.

The Avanti was Studebaker's last clean-sheet car, and as last gasps go, it was a beaut. The body combined curves and angles in such a fresh, modern way that the car looked radical in 1963—and thoroughly up to date years later, as succeeding companies proved when they continued to produce it.

A small, skilled group assembled by the famed industrial designer Raymond Loewy penned the flowing shape. Long praised for his work in shaping the European elegance of Studebaker's early 1950s coupes, especially the 1953, Loewy's firm hadn't worked on a South Bend design since 1956. But with the Avanti, it was evident that Loewy had not lost his touch. Commissioned as a sporty attention-getter and a vision of the future for Studebaker, the design evolved in an improba-

The 1962 GT Hawk was the final redesign of Studebaker's stunning "Loewy coupe" first shown in 1953. Originally a Portland, Oregon, car, the Hawk in these photos spent most of its life in California before heading to Troy, New York, with its current owner, John Reichard.

bly short time. The first full-scale mock-up was completed in just over a month.

All Avantis rode on a chopped version of the Lark convertible frame. The suspension was suitably upgraded to be worthy of the shape, and serious Bendix disk brakes appeared at the front. On the inside, a padded dash, safety cone door locks, and a built-in rollbar presaged federal standards by years. Several versions of Studebaker's venerable 289-inch V-8 could be found under the hood, rang-

ing from 240 to as much as 335 horsepower (with supercharging).

Studebaker's financial straits lent a certain urgency to the Avanti project while simultaneously posing some practical constraints. To save time and money, the body would be fashioned out of fiberglass—a decision that would later haunt the company when problems developed with the outsourced shells. The first batch of wavy bodies could (literally) not be straightened out in time for the original production deadlines, and this delay cost the Avanti dearly. Already wary of South Bend's weakening financial health, the postponed rollout further spooked would-be buyers.

Avanti sales never took off. Only 3,834 units were produced in the first year, followed by 809 in 1964. Thus, despite its futuristic lines and sparkling performance, the Avanti couldn't save its ailing parent—in truth, probably *nothing* could. When Studebaker headed north of the border to complete its final two years of production in Canada, the sleek but unprofitable Avanti didn't follow.

After Studebaker died, the Avanti was revived by a series of small firms and continued being produced on and off for decades. Under Studebaker's aegis it had only lasted two years, but that was enough to provide a brash legacy and a final, emphatic period on the story that Studebaker had been writing since 1902.

Studebaker Hawk
Flying High on Borrowed Time

While Raymond Loewy and his crew were developing the Avanti, another designer was toiling away at an equally daunting task. Brooks Stevens had the unenviable job of giving Studebaker's Hawk and Lark facelifts on a low-buck budget and under-the-gun time frame. Stevens pulled off the improbable—he cleanly restyled the Lark and virtually reinvented the Hawk.

The Hawk was Studebaker's "Family Sports Car." First appearing in 1956, it was based on the beautifully simple 1953 Starliner coupe, a styling—though not sales—sensation. The Hawk kept the Starliner's long, low profile and added an inverted trapezoid grille—a styling calling card of every Hawk to follow.

For the rest of the 1950s, the Hawk was Studebaker's style and performance leader. Yet

The Flame Red GT Hawk coupe boasts a number of interesting options including factory four-speed, Twin Traction, Climatizer, reclining buckets, and heavy-duty springs.

despite feeding the public a steady diet of looks, luxury, and performance, buyers never warmed to it. As the new decade began, Hawk sales were hitting their lowest point to date, dipping under 4,000 units for 1960.

The following year, Sherwood Egbert took the helm at Studebaker and rolled up his sleeves. Egbert brought Raymond Loewy back into the fold and gave him the task of creating a new car—and a new vision—for the company, which resulted in the Avanti. At the same time, Brooks Stevens got the job of taking care of the present. Specifically, Stevens was to re-do the Lark and Hawk. Both birds benefited from their new plumage, and the Hawk's feathers proved particularly pleasing.

The new-for-1962 Gran Turismo Hawk had its wings clipped in back, with rounded, rectangular fenders replacing the former canted fins. Up front, a much cleaner bumper and less-conflicting trim underscored the classic semi-trapezoidal grille. The side view was particularly striking: The thick roofline was obviously lifted from the Thunderbird, but the clean profile was wonderfully unfettered by

For a while, the sensible size and economy of the Lark helped Studebaker tread water in a sea of red ink. But while practicality was at the heart of every compact, that didn't mean buyers didn't want some fun along the way. One year after its 1959 introduction the Lark came out in ragtop form. While timing had the most to do with the Lark's early success, the car's chunky, cute styling didn't hurt—this one's a 1961.

brightwork, save the ribbed rocker panels. The overall effect was stunning—a tasteful, timeless shape crafted from what was now a ten-year-old body. That Stevens was able to summon such a gracious design from the resources at hand must be considered as one of the great styling achievements of all time.

The new Hawk still carried Studebaker's 289 V-8, a capable performer despite its girth. Four-barrel models were rated at 225 horsepower, enough for creditable, if not brilliant, acceleration. The crisp restyle more than doubled sales, and 9,335 Hawks were built in 1962. Sadly, the trend couldn't be sustained. Sales swooped again (to 4,634) in 1963 and a paltry 1,767 in 1964, the Hawk's final year. Worries over finances hung over the once-proud car maker like a fog, all but obscuring the appeal of the Hawk, Lark, and Avanti from the public. As the company's fortunes grew darker, consumer confidence ebbed, and buyers found fewer and fewer reasons to abandon the security of the Big Three—even if it was tempting.

And that's a shame, because the final Hawks *were* tempting cars. Many things about them, including their styling, appointments, and performance, foreshadowed the more successful cars that followed. Though the 1958 Thunderbird is usually credited with creating the personal-luxury market and the Mustang is called the first pony car, a careful check of their lineage would reveal more than a little Hawk.

Studebaker Lark

Life's a Lark—Until They Repossess the Nest

As if redesigning one car under the gun and on a shoestring wouldn't have been enough, Brooks Stevens had two to contend with for the 1962 model year: the sporty Hawk and the compact Lark. Appearing in 1959, the Lark had been a savior for South Bend, providing a welcome infusion of cash at a time when success was in short supply. Alas, the Lark only provided a stay of execution, not a pardon, for Studebaker. But for one brief moment at least there had been hope.

For Studebaker, the compact Lark was the automotive equivalent of a finger in the dike. It plugged the leak for a while, but eventually the wall crumbled, and the proud company washed away.

While no auto maker had a good year in recession-ravaged 1958, Studebaker was hit particularly hard. During that year the company finally threw in the towel and ended Packard production—just as well, perhaps, since the 1957-1958 models were merely Packard/Studebaker hybrids that ill-served both marques.

But while Packard was dead by 1959, Studebaker wasn't feeling much better. Sales had slid to just 44,759 units in 1958, putting the marque in a dismal 14th place for the industry. South Bend wasn't finished yet, though, and in 1959 the company came charging back. Having discarded the entire 1958 lineup except for the Hawk, Studebaker unveiled a new compact called the Lark and promptly sold 131,078 of them. That (and 7,788 Hawks) brought Studie up to 11th in the industry and elevated the patient's status from "critical" to just "serious."

Compacts weren't entirely unheard of in 1959—the Rambler and Volkswagen continued selling well—but 1958's economic downturn helped fuel interest in smaller, more economical cars, so the Lark just happened to walk out on stage to find that it was playing to a packed house. The low-volume Hawk aside, Larks represented the entire Studebaker lineup for 1959. As such, they were offered in a full range of body styles: two- and four-door sedans and a two-door wagon with six- or eight-cylinder power. For 1959 the Lark and Rambler pretty much had the field to themselves, but in 1960 the Big Three came charging in with Corvair, Falcon, and Valiant, effectively ending the party. The Lark still sold well in 1960, and the addition of a four-door wagon and ragtop (the only one in the class for the moment) added lots of appeal. But all that new competition from auto makers with far deeper pockets and much bigger dealer networks spelled trouble ahead.

Nineteen sixty-two brought the second of Stevens' quick-fix makeovers. The Lark graduated from cute to classier, with a broader, beveled grille, squared shoulders, and longer rear fenders capped by circular taillights. It was a good look, and buyers responded to the tune of an almost a 40 percent sales increase. But the surge was short lived: Studebaker's fiscal woes scared off a lot of buyers in 1963, and even the debut of the Avanti could do little to calm their fears. By year's end, the South Bend facility would be shuttered and production exiled to Canada, where an emasculated lineup was produced for two more years. In March 1966, the last Studebaker rolled off the assembly line at Hamilton, Ontario.

| The Lark Daytona Hardtop | The Lark Wagonaire | The Hawk |

meet America's first cars with the feel and features of tomorrow

Today, you may win an advanced '63 car from Studebaker. If you do, you'll recognize instantly how far into the future Studebaker has moved.

Superchargers. Disc Brakes with remarkable stopping power. Stop quicker, straighter, smoother than with ordinary brakes under any conditions. There's a built-in Ladies' Vanity, new interiors, bucket seats, 4-speed

'63 *AVANTI* America's Most Advanced Automobile
'63 *LARK* The Feature Car of Its Class
'63 *CRUISER* America's First and Only Limousette
'63 *HAWK* America's Popular Priced Sports Classic

gear boxes. The Avanti, Lark, Wagonaire, Hawk and Cruiser are something dramatically new in automobiles—because each is designed to meet the <u>different</u> requirements of the family, the luxury lover, the performance-minded. Each is a car with a purpose.

Why not discover the Drive of the Future at a **Studebaker Dealer's Showroom?**

FROM THE ADVANCED THINKING OF

Studebaker
CORPORATION

With the Lark, Hawk, and Avanti, Studebaker was hardly wanting for products in 1963. Unfortunately, fewer and fewer buyers were willing to consider the South Bend, Indiana, independent as word of its dire financial straits got around. Neat as they were, the Lark's fabric sunroof and the Lark Wagonaire's retractable metal top were notorious leakers, and the money simply wasn't there to engineer a proper fix.

Visually just a Rambler American with cool wheels, a funky hood, and a decidedly patriotic paint job, the SC/Rambler was actually an effective muscle collaboration between AMC and the performance specialists at Hurst. A healthy, ram-air-fed 390 motivated this bargain-priced musclecar, which cost just $2,998 out the door. Two versions of the Fourth of July paint scheme were offered; the flashier "A" version (shown) made it onto 1,512 cars.

AMC High Performance

Anybody who wanted to do battle with the Big Three in the mid- to late 1960s had to have credible musclecars. AMC did it with such models as the shoebox-styled SC Rambler and the more purposefully shaped AMX.

Like the singles hitter who can't resist swinging for the fences, American Motors had an irresistible urge to stray beyond its proven success in compacts and take on the Big Three across the board. It can be argued that this strategy was the single biggest factor in the company's demise—but while it lasted,

How to tell a Marlin '66 from any other sports fastback.

Put your family in it.

(Even with "buckets" this fastback
seats six—in comfort. Read #3 below.)

'66 Marlin

An ungainly treatment of the Tarpon showcar's fastback theme, the first-generation Marlin floundered for AMC.

82

the approach sure brought out some interesting products.

Despite its frugal roots, it's interesting to note that AMC was one of the true pioneers of the musclecar with the little-known 1957 Rambler Rebel. Just 1,500 of these special silver-and-gold four-doors were built, all powered by a 327 V-8 good for 255 horsepower and capable of 0 to 60 in the mid-sevens.

Some of AMC's first and last musclecars of the 1960s were also Rambler-based, and one of the best was the Hurst SC/Rambler built in 1969. The "Scramblers" were painted in either of two hard-to-miss red-white-and-blue color schemes. Lurking behind these patriotic shoebox looks was serious musclecar hardware: A 390 V-8 good for 325 brake horsepower coupled to a four-speed gearbox and a 3.54:1 rear end. The result could turn low-14 quarters right out of the box.

Scramblers aside, the hottest AMCs were the 2+2 Javelin and two-seat Javelin-based AMX. The Javelin was one of the last entries in the 1960s pony car race. Introduced in model year 1968, it was produced through 1974. The option list offered two engines capable of flinging this machine down the highway quite nicely, a 343-inch V-8 and an even stronger 390. A couple of interesting models were spun off of the Javelin, including the SST Trans-Am. Another Javelin of note was the Mark Donohue Signature Edition, which sported a fat ducktail spoiler and a functional ram-air hood scoop. Some 2,501 Donohue models were produced, honoring the racing exploits of the AMC team member.

The AMX, meanwhile, was a Javelin-based two-seater of considerable charm and strength. Introduced in 1968, the AMX rode on a sawed-off Javelin platform with a 97-inch wheelbase and a 290-cid standard V-8 engine. The 343- and 390-cubic inch engines were available optionally, the latter capable of ushering the AMX from 0 to 60 in under seven seconds. If that wasn't enough to convince the cognoscenti, AMC hired the famous Craig Breedlove to set over 100 speed-and-distance records with the AMX in February 1968.

Alas, the AMX's life span was as short as its wheelbase. Launched in late February 1968, it disappeared after the 1970 model year. Just over 19,000 were sold in its brief but memorable production run.

American Motors Marlin
Part Pony car, Part Draft Horse

Auto styles, like other styles, fall in and out of favor. Fastbacks were in fashion in the 1940s, but had pretty much disappeared by the early 1950s. The body style re-emerged with a vengeance in the 1960s. Among the most notable examples were the Plymouth Barracuda, Dodge Charger, Ford Mustang, and AMC Marlin.

Fastbacks and pony cars were two 1960s trends that occasionally existed together. The sweeping roofline that defines the fastback was carried off with varying degrees of success during the decade, especially with the large, first-generation versions of the emerging fastback class: The 1966–1967 Dodge Charger and 1965–1966 Rambler/AMC Marlin. While dramatic, their proportions never looked quite *right*.

The Marlin popped into the Rambler lineup in 1965, based on a concept car named the Tarpon, which had hit the circuit a year earlier. But while the Tarpon's tidy proportions were nicely scaled to its 106-inch wheelbase, the Marlin was a bigger fish. In a classic case of misguided one-upmanship, AMC decided that if a 2+2 was good, then a 3+3 must be better. The basic Tarpon concept was therefore stretched to handle three-across seating front and rear, landing the body on the Rambler's midsized Classic chassis.

Like another fish—Plymouth's Barracuda—the Marlin was spawned without knowledge of the upcoming pony car boom. Soon after birth, though, it got caught up in those currents while still learning to swim. The Marlin became AMC's *de facto* Mustang fighter simply because nothing else came close. A menu of sporty options included three V-8s, a four-speed stick, and a tach. The six-passenger seating was also convenient, but it came at the cost of storage space. Worse still, the small trunk couldn't be reached via a fold-down rear seat as in some of the competition. First-year sales of 10,327 were followed by an even more paltry 4,547 units in 1966—the year that the Rambler nameplate was replaced outright by the American Motors badge.

The Marlin's cumbersome styling was revamped in 1967. The second-generation car was stretched out even more than the first, this time to fit the Ambassador series' 118-inch wheelbase. The new treatment had better symmetry and proportions, so even though it was bigger, the new Marlin looked cleaner than its predecessor. But in heading upstream to look for sustenance, the Marlin had little success. Sales slowed to just 2,545 for the year, and AMC pulled the plug. Its replacement was the on-the-money Javelin. Javelin not only gave AMC a credible competitor in the pony car ranks, it also provided the basic platform from which the company launched its most serious musclecar, the AMX.

Rambler American
Last of the Legacy

Compacts were Rambler/AMC's bread and butter, and the company's focus on them was the root of its greatest success in the late 1950s/early 1960s. The later decision to abandon this strategy and try to build something for everyone paved the way for the company's demise.

The first Rambler appeared in 1950 as a small-car alternative to the rest of the Nash line, but Ramblers later became the core product of the company that would come to be known as American Motors. This happened in 1957, when the last remnants of the Nash and Hudson lines were dropped. Rambler had the good fortune to enter the 1958 market with precisely the right cars for the times. A vicious recession hit that year, and the inexpensive Rambler tallied up profits of $26,000,000.

A big part of the Rambler's late 1950s success was having the right product at the right time. But another factor was a lack of competition, which didn't last long. When the 1960 Ramblers took the field, they faced not only Studebaker's Lark (which appeared in 1959) but also new offerings from Chevy, Plymouth, and Ford (soon joined by Mercury). The next year things got even more crowded as new small cars appeared from Buick, Olds, and Pontiac.

Rambler's basic compact became known as the American in 1960, a name it would keep until 1969. Throughout the decade the American was Rambler's key car, but management had bigger ideas. After company president George Romney left AMC in early 1962 to campaign (successfully) for the governorship of Michigan, his successor, Roy Abernethy, began steering the firm toward head-to-head, across-the-board competition with the Big Three.

As the base compact in the lineup, the American's sales remained steady through the first half of the 1960s, regularly exceeding 100,000 units. On the downside of the decade, though, the numbers began to decline. Still, it's interesting to note that production of the American and the slightly larger Classic—the cars closest to the original Rambler concept—remained AMC's best sellers.

The American nameplate was dropped after 1968, and AMC built its last car in model year 1987, leaving in its wake one of autodom's enduring questions. If AMC had stuck with its strengths and resisted the urge to expand, would there still be an American independent?

AMBASSADOR

The Red Carpet Ride.
Now—this rich driving experience is yours in an uncompromising selection of full-size automobiles. From $2515 to $3143.*

THE NOW CARS FROM THE 1967 AMERICAN MOTORS
AMBASSADOR · MARLIN · REBEL · RAMBLER AMERICAN

The Ambassador was a full-sized line from a company known for compacts. In an effort to distinguish them from the rest of the Ramblers, the Ambassadors got bigger starting in 1965. Initially bigger meant better, at least in terms of sales. The 64,000-plus Ambassadors sold in 1965 was the best showing this nameplate had seen to date. The 1967 models sported a clean new shape, courtesy of AMC design boss Dick Teague, the master of shoe-string-budget styling. Riding a decidedly noncompact 118-inch wheelbase, the Ambassador coupled a Ford-like roof and Rambleresque nose in a package that looked trimmer than it was. The 1967 Ambassador was big, smooth, and safe, but it didn't sell as well as it deserved to—something that could be said for many AMC products in the 1960s and 1970s. The Ambassador, like the Javelin, was dropped after 1974.

6

Pickup Trucks and Station Wagons

For decades, pickup trucks and station wagons were always considered utilitarian vehicles, nothing more than simple modes of conveyance for cargo and large families. They were rough, Spartan, and underpowered. But toward the end of the 1950s, when they both received flashy mechanical and styling refinements, they gained a higher acceptance among the general car-buying public. When the 1960s arrived, they were considered mainstream, just like a two-door hardtop or four-door sedan. Pickups now had more power and personal conveniences, and the station wagons became luxurious family cars.

Pickups

Pickups have always sold well in this country; why may be open to debate. Some argue that Americans love our wild west cowboy heritage, and the pickup is the spiritual successor to the horse. Others say they just need something that'll carry a load from the building supply store. But whether for poetic reasons or practical ones, pickups remain popular.

Ford Ranchero
Having It Both Ways

One trend that caught on again in the late 1950s and carried through the 1960s was the car/truck hybrid. Part workhorse, part clothes horse, these trucks sought to combine the best of two worlds for people who liked a car's looks, ride, and comfort but sometimes needed a truck.

Chevy's El Camino and Ford's Ranchero weren't the only hybrid car/trucks of the 1960s. Studebaker's entry was the Champ. But where the Ford and Chevy were more car than truck, the Studie was just the opposite. Essentially a Lark-based body on an existing truck chassis, they were produced from 1960 through the start of model year 1964. Studebaker had more experience with such hybrids than any of its competition—the swoopy Coupe-Express of 1937–1938 was one of the pioneers of the field. Studebaker added a wide-body option in 1961 and minor upgrades (improved steering, suspension, an available five-speed) and creature comforts over the next few years. Regrettably, the last Champ Pickup was built two days after Christmas 1963.

By 1968 the Ranchero was in its second full season as a Fairlane-based intermediate. This was a restyle year, and the Ranchero traded its stacked 1967 headlights for side-by-side quads in 1968. Government-mandated side marker lights appeared the same year, and the glass was reworked to eliminate vent windows. Base, 500, and GT versions sold 5,014, 10,029, and 1,669 units, respectively, in 1968.

Ford didn't invent the car/truck; what the Ranchero did was popularize the idea and bring it into the mainstream. The dual-use vehicle had been around for decades before the Ranchero in the form of the Studebaker Coupe-Express and Hudson Sedan Pickup, to name just two. Then Ford revived the idea in 1957 with what was essentially a sawed-off Ford Ranch Wagon with some finishing modifications. All the 1957 Fords were good looking, and the Ranchero shared in this virtue, looking especially low and sleek against the standard high, boxy light trucks of the day.

Throughout its life, the Ranchero followed the trends of the line on which it was based. This policy had good and bad points. Ford's rather weak 1958 and 1959 styling meant a less attractive Ranchero, too. And when the company got small with the Falcon in 1960, the Ranchero went along for the ride. If for no other reason than to allow the use of this metaphor, sales of the Falcon-based Ranchero took flight that year, jumping about 30 percent over the full-sized 1959s. The Ranchero stayed tied to the Falcon through 1965, and production hovered in a remarkably even band at around 20,000 units per year from 1960 to 1963. When the Falcon's styling changed in 1964 (and not for the better), Ranchero sales fell nearly in half.

The Ranchero's third life began in 1966, when the little car/truck began morphing into a Fairlane pickup. The 1966 versions retained the Falcon's beak but rode on a Fairlane chassis, and by 1967 the transformation was complete: The Ranchero, which started life on a

When the Chevelle got a fresh look in 1966, so did the El Camino—any styling tweaks done to one were automatically carried to the other. As the 1960s wore on, more and more drivetrains became available in the El Camino. By 1966, two dozen different engine/transmission combos could be had, from a 194 cubic-inch manual-shift six to a 396-cubic-inch-displacement V-8 with Turbo Hydra-Matic. This black beauty is equipped with Chevy's classic 327 small-block.

full-sized chassis and downsized straight to a compact, now assumed the dimensions of an intermediate.

For the rest of the decade, the Ranchero's development mirrored that of the Fairlane. In keeping with the times, that meant it could be had with an ever-expanding list of luxury and high-performance options. What began the decade as "America's Lowest Priced Pickup" (just $1,882) powered by a 90-horse straight-six ended the 1960s with a base price of $2,623, a standard 155-horsepower six, and optional engines all the way up to a 335-brake horsepower 428 Cobra Jet.

But the Ranchero had one more transformation up its sleeve. From the early 1970s through its last year of production (1979), the truck was based on the Torino. This model took over as Ford's resident intermediate series in 1971 after beginning life as the top trim level of the Fairlane. The Torino-based trucks lacked the snappy styling of earlier generations, and this combined with the growing influence of small imported pickups to further shrink the Ranchero's market. By the end of the 1970s, the time had come to be gone.

Chevrolet El Camino
Half and Half, Chevy Style

The world wasn't bereft of sporty pickups before the Ranchero. In 1955, Chevy introduced the classy Cameo Carrier and its GMC counterpart, the Suburban. Two years later, Dodge brought out the first finned pickup, the D100 Sweptside. But after Ford released its car-based Ranchero that same year, Chevy responded with the El Camino for 1959.

As the styling for their parent cars went, so went the car/truck hybrids. This simple fact dictated that the first El Caminos would look like the 1959 Chevy—which is to say *bizarre*. The 1959 Chevys were known for their big chrome eyebrows and broad, flat batwing fins, but for some reason these didn't look as outrageous on the El Camino as they did on the regular cars. The pickup returned in 1960 wearing Chevy's toned-down take on the flamboyant 1959s, but it dropped out thereafter while Ford's Ranchero evolved into a compact car/truck. After a breather, the El Camino returned to the fray in 1964, now based on the Chevelle.

It was an interesting turnaround. The El Camino was a response to the Ranchero, and as such Ford had a two-year jump on building market identity. But when Chevy's entry returned from its self-imposed hiatus, it was as an intermediate—which beat the Ranchero to that step by two years. This, coupled with Ford's rather bland 1964 styling, gave the born-again El Camino a run on the rest of the decade. Its 1964 sales easily outstripped its rival's, and Chevy backed up that success with the addition of more under-hood firepower, like a solid-lifter 327 V-8 pushing out 350 horsepower. In 1966, the Chevelle was restyled, so the El Camino enjoyed sleeker looks too. At the same time a Super Sport package became available featuring special trim and performance enhancements.

El Camino development followed the Chevelle for the rest of the decade. The Chevelle's 1968 restyle made for a longer and taller pickup that year, and aside from annual tweaks, the looks remained largely unchanged from 1968 through 1972. The same wasn't true for output, though, and when this began slipping in 1971, the El Camino found it was indeed a slippery slope. Performance-wise, the high-water mark for both the El Camino SS and Ford Ranchero GT was probably 1970. That year both pickups offered a hard-to-resist combination of muscle-car performance and striking car/truck styling. Like the Ranchero, Chevy's El Camino proved durable in the marketplace. The Ranchero exited after 1979, but Chevy's entry soldiered on through 1987.

Station Wagons

The 1960s were probably the last blast for station wagons. Gas shortages in the 1970s forced downsizing, while the 1980s brought us the minivan and the resurgence of sport-utility vehicles, both of which directly poached on wagon buyers. But back in the 1960s, wagons were big—in more ways than one.

Oldsmobile Vista Cruiser
Through the Glass Tinted

The long station-wagon trip is the stuff of childhood memories, and the 1960s was its heyday. But wagons came in all styles and sizes, and one of the most interesting will always be the Vista Cruiser.

Arriving fashionably late to Oldsmobile's 1964 lineup was a surprise called the Vista Cruiser—a glass-laden, intermediate-class wagon that formally debuted at the Chicago Auto Show. The Vista Cruiser was a well-built, well-dressed machine

Vista-Cruiser by **OLDSMOBILE**

OLDSMOBILE DIVISION • GENERAL MOTORS CORP.

Destination: New York World's Fair
Transportation: World's newest Station Wagon!

Leave it to Olds to put extra fun in fair-going! Leave it to
Vista-Cruiser to prove the point! Here's a see-all, carry-all wagon
that's brand new from Vista-Roof above to vanishing road below!
Up front, it's all action with up to 290 horses to do the honors.
Down under, it's all ride with a 10-foot wheelbase and four coil springs
to keep you on the level! *Inside,* it's all space . . . over 100 cubic feet
in both two- and three-seat models (third seat faces forward, too!).
And in the rear? Just miles and miles of highway you've left behind!
Look to Olds for all that's new . . . drive the all-new Vista-Cruiser!

'64 OLDS *WHERE THE ACTION IS!*

SEE ALL THE QUALITY-
BUILT 1964 OLDSMOBILES
AT THE OLDS EXHIBIT:
Ninety-Eight, Starfire,
Super 88, Dynamic 88,
Jetstar I, Jetstar 88, F-85

most notable for its novel, windowed roofline. Fixed, tinted skylights surrounded back-seat passengers and gave the cars a distinctly lighter look, both inside and out.

The classy, glassy Olds sold well in its first full year (1965), and it returned in 1966 as a distinct model on a 120-inch wheelbase. The Vista Cruiser would remain Oldsmobile's top wagon line through the end of the decade, offering two- and three-bench versions with 100-plus cubic feet of cargo space. This largest of Olds wagons gradually gained weight as the decade wore on. By 1969, it was closer to a battleship than a cruiser, with the three-bench model tipping the scales at more than 2 tons and costing some $3,600. The familiar name dropped off the charts after 1977.

Studebaker Lark Wagonaire
"America's Most Unusual Wagon"

Despite an increasingly gloomy prognosis for survival, Studebaker developed one more innovative take on an old standby during the 1960s: the Lark Wagonaire of 1963-1966.

With two notable Studebaker successes to his credit (the restyled Lark and Hawk), industrial designer Brooks Stevens also gets some of the blame for a notable Studebaker failure—the Lark Wagonaire. The premise was simple and quite utilitarian: The Wagonaire was a basic cargo hauler with one simple twist: a retractable rear roof section to allow greater cargo hauling options. Studebaker marketed it as part convertible (presumably the *rear* part), part sedan, and part utility wagon.

The roof did indeed slide open; the trouble was what happened when it slid *shut*. The Wagonaire's roof panel proved hopelessly leak prone, and even-

tually rust prone as well. Realizing that something was amiss, Studebaker interrupted production early on and tried to find a fix, but it was soon decided that the money required to solve the problem was more than Studebaker had. The line started rolling again, and all Wagonaires were simply at risk of taking on water. To hedge its bets, Studebaker quickly reintroduced a conventional fixed-roof wagon for $100 less.

Because of their novelty (and soon their reputation for cargo-bay incontinence), the Wagonaire never really caught on. In many ways its concept of multipurpose utility presaged the popularity of today's sport-utility vehicles, especially the station wagon/SUV hybrids. But because the money wasn't there to make the thing work, Stevens' Wagonaire was destined to be remembered as a watershed design that couldn't shed water.

In 1978 and 1979, the fastest-accelerating American production vehicle was a truck, not a car—which probably says more about the sorry state of cars at the time than it does about the quickness of this pickup. Even so, the truck in question was Dodge's Li'l Red Express, an over-the-top version of the Adventurer D150. The Canyon Red truck—its beautiful oak trim counterpointed by outlandish gold graphics—was brash, loud, and *quick*, thanks to a high-output 360-inch Dodge V-8 and 3.55:1 axle ratio. Some 5,118 examples were produced in 1979, the last year of the Express.

7

Into the 1970s

The 1970s started much like the 1960s. High-performance cars enjoyed perhaps their finest year ever in 1970, with memorable 11th-hour contributions to the musclecar hall of fame being made by every U.S. manufacturer.

Things were about to change, however, and cars soon sank into a period of doldrums from which they wouldn't fully emerge until the mid-1980s. Rising insurance costs, the need for energy conservation, and government safety and pollution mandates all conspired to shift the direction of auto making quickly and dramatically. Worse still, when the Arab oil embargo flared up, Americans were forced to do something that they had not done since World War II: wait in line for gas.

The insurance/energy backlash had real and immediate consequences in the showroom. To meet new emissions and consumption realities, compression ratios dropped (taking lots of horsepower with them), and musclecars dried up like puddles in the noonday sun. Not surprisingly, the 1970s also brought renewed interest in economy cars. American auto makers struggled to keep up with the market, continuing to build big cars but rushing to create small ones as well. Large autos got progressively smaller, but also less satisfying. Powered by emasculated small-blocks and V-6s, the full-sized cars were anemic, while Detroit's economy models generally achieved their decent miles per gallon at the price of value and build

quality. Cars such as the Ford Pinto and Chevy Vega came and went during the decade, and few seemed sorry to see them go.

The beneficiaries of all of this (aside from OPEC) were the import manufacturers who made a full-scale assault on the American market in the 1970s armed with miserly gas mileage and enviable reliability. The big Japanese firms in particular benefited from the changing times. Toyota and Datsun (Nissan) were car companies known to few in the 1960s, but in the 1970s, they—and increasingly Honda—became widely known and much sought after. Demand exceeded supply, and waiting lists were created for the most popular models.

The 1970s exacted a sort of Jurassic revenge: The cars that ate the most fossil fuels in the 1960s suddenly became dinosaurs themselves. American carmakers would rebound, but it was well into the 1980s before customers saw the first hard evidence that Detroit had learned the essential truth of the times: Value is as much about quality as it is about price.

In cars, as in culture, the further the 1960s recede from us, the more difficult it is to believe the way we were. Did we really drive cars that huge? Did gas ever cost that little? Did people really think that their hair looked good like that? Yes, yes, and yes. Times were just *different* then.

Index